WAR PLANES OF THE SECOND WORLD WAR

FIGHTERS

VOLUME THREE

WILLIAM GREEN

With Drawings by Dennis I. Punnett

MACDONALD : LONDON

© William Green, 1961

First published in 1961 by
Macdonald & Co., (Publishers) Ltd.
16 Maddox Street, W.1
Made and Printed in Great Britain by
Purnell and Sons, Ltd.
Paulton (Somerset) and London

INTRODUCTION

A major enigma in the years immediately preceding the Second World War was the quality of the air forces of Japan and the Soviet Union. Both nations were popularly believed to be copyists and regarded qualitatively if not quantitatively as second-class air powers; their aircraft being out-dated by world standards and largely derived from obsolescent European or American designs. Neither the Sino-Japanese conflict nor the Spanish Civil War in which Russian warplanes were employed extensively on behalf of the Republican government presented any evidence to contradict these beliefs. However, the first weeks of the Pacific War revealed all too dramatically how seriously we in the West had underrated the capabilities of Japanese aircraft designers, and while the German assault on the Soviet Union six months previously had not uncovered such startling revelations, the conflict on the Eastern Front soon disclosed the fact that the Soviet aircraft industry could produce competent warplanes ideally suited to the operational conditions existing in Russia.

In this volume, the fighters and fighter-bombers of both Japan and the Soviet Union are described and illustrated. For many years prior to the war, the J.A.A.F. and J.N.A.F. had been firm adherents of the classic dog-fighting methods of fighter-versus-fighter combat and, thus, considered manœuvrability to be of paramount importance. The fighters with which Japan entered the war placed emphasis on extreme manœuvrability; speed, armour protection and fire-power all being subordinated to the Japanese pilot's demand for a standard of manœuvrability long since foregone in favour of other qualities by western designers. This policy appeared to have been justified during the early stages of the Pacific War, but as the Allies began to take the measure of the Japanese fighters the J.A.A.F. and J.N.A.F. demanded greater speed, heavier armament and some protection for the pilot and fuel tanks, these qualities finally taking precedence over extreme manœuvrability. In consequence, as the war progressed, the Japanese produced some highly sophisticated fighters, comparing favourably with the best produced by the Allies.

The Soviet aircraft industry produced less sophisticated fighters than those of the other warring nations, quantity taking precedence over quality. Production was concentrated on a few types of relatively simple design. Short of light alloys, the Russians made extensive use of wood and steel-tube in their fighters, and little attention was given to detail refinement. Without exception, the fighters serving with the Soviet Air Forces were completely ortho-dox, multi-purpose machines, rugged, depend-able and simply equipped, but despite the exigencies of the times, Russian designers did not ignore the development of less orthodox fighters for more specialised roles, although none of these succeeded in attaining service status. While details of most of these experi-mental Russian fighters are included in the following pages, details of at least three types, the rocket-powered Polikarpov Malyutka and Tikhonravov 302 and the twin-engined Moskalov SAM-13, remain obscure.

In conclusion, I should like to record my indebtedness to H. Somberg, B. van der Klaauw, Richard M. Bueschel, Eiichiro Sekigawa, Jacques Marmain, J. S. Orwovski and J. B. Cynk, all of whom have supplied information for inclusion in this volume.

London, January 1961   William Green

KAWANISHI N1K1-J SHIDEN (GEORGE 11) JAPAN

The Kawanishi Kokuki K.K., which had completed and flown the first prototype of the 15-*Shi* Kyofu (Mighty Wind) float fighter in August 1942, began work on a landplane adaptation of the floatplane in November 1942 to meet J.N.A.F. requirements for an interceptor fighter for operation from land bases. Known as the Model X-1 Shiden (Violet Lightning), the first prototype was completed some nine months later, in July 1943, and, possessing a basically similar airframe to that of the Kyofu floatplane, was powered by a 1,990 h.p. Nakajima NK9H Homare 21. This engine had been placed in production before the completion of final tests and, in consequence, it was plagued with teething troubles.

The Shiden was a compromise between rapid produceability and operational requirements. One of the most difficult problems facing the design staff in its development had been the provision of a retractable undercarriage of adequate length to permit the use of an airscrew of sufficient diameter to make full use of the available power yet fit within the limitations of the mid-wing configuration. Legs of exceptional length had to be adopted, and to stow these units in the wings a system of double retraction had to be evolved. The legs were lowered and then extended, and when retracting they contracted as they folded into the wing wells. Flight trials soon revealed that the Shiden possessed outstanding manoeuvrability, a feature due in no small part to its "combat" flaps which changed their angle automatically with changes in *g* value during manoeuvres, supplying additional surface when a high lift coefficient was required.

Prior to the first flight trials, the Shiden had been ordered into production off the drawing board. Three further prototypes were completed before the end of July 1943, and full

4

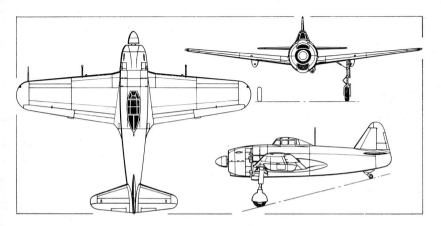

production was attained less than a year after the fighter's inception. Five more prototypes were produced, and the testing of these proceeded concurrently with that of the first production N1K1-J Shiden Type B Fighter, Model 11. The rapidity with which the new fighter had reached production status had not allowed sufficient time in which to eliminate the teething troubles that soon appeared in the prototypes, however, and the production lines were continually inflicted with design changes and modifications dictated by flight testing.

Production of the N1K1-J was initiated by Kawanishi's Naruo plant, but, in December 1943, it also entered production at the Himeji factory. From July until the end of 1943, the Naruo plant produced seventy N1K1-J fighters, building a further 465 by December 1944 when production was phased out in favour of the improved Shiden-Kai. One Shiden was produced at Himeji in December 1943, and a further 467 had been completed when U.S. bombing brought production to a halt. Thus, a total of 1,007 N1K1-J fighters, including prototypes, were built.

Three basic production models of the N1K1-J Shiden fighter were built, these differing principally in the arrangement of the armament. The original N1K1-J had two 7.7-mm. guns in the fuselage, two 20-mm. cannon in the wings and two 20-mm. cannon suspended under the wings in gondolas. The N1K1-Ja Shiden 11a had the 7.7-mm. guns deleted, and the N1K1-Jb Shiden 11b had a modified wing structure permitting all four cannon to be installed internally in the wings. Late production N1K1-Jb fighters had completely redesigned, square-tipped vertical tail surfaces. Another late modification was the fitting of six rocket-powered bombs on a rack beneath

(Above and below) A standard N1K1-J Shiden prior to installation of wing cannon.

This close-up of the N1K1-J (below) shows the starboard cannon and ejector exhausts.

the fuselage. One Shiden 11 was modified late in 1944 to take a supplementary rocket boost unit beneath the rear fuselage as the N1K1-J-KAI. Several machines were later modified in a similar fashion as a result of the encouraging results of flight tests, but the rocket-boosted Shiden never attained operational service.

The Shiden entered service with the J.N.A.F. early in 1944, and despite troubles with its Homare engine and shortcomings resulting from the inadequate development period, it soon proved itself a redoubtable warplane, and its pilots came to look upon the formidable Grumman Hellcat as a relatively easy "kill". The Shiden 11 was first met in numbers over Formosa and the Philippines, the first Shiden-equipped unit to oppose U.S. forces being the 341st Air Corps which arrived at Luzon from Formosa on October 20, 1944 as part of the J.N.A.F. 2nd Air Fleet. The Shiden 11 was again met in large numbers during the invasion of Okinawa, and was encountered frequently until the end of the war, by which time a number of fighters of this type had been expended in suicide attacks. In fact, a specially modified version of the Shiden was intended for the suicide-attack role but no production of the suicide variant was undertaken and it was not used operationally.

Type: *Single-seat Interceptor Fighter and Fighter-bomber.* **Power Plant:** *One 1,990 h.p. Nakajima NK9H Homare 21 eighteen-cylinder radial air-cooled engine.* **Armament:** *Two 7.7-mm. Type 97 machine guns and four 20-mm. Type 99 cannon.* **Performance:** *Maximum speed, 362 m.p.h. at 17,715 ft., 334 m.p.h. at 9,840 ft.; range, 888 mls. at 230 m.p.h. at 13,120 ft.; time to 19,685 ft., 7 min. 50 sec.; service ceiling, 39,700 ft.* **Weights:** *Empty, 5,598 lb.; loaded, 9,526 lb.* **Dimensions:** *Span, 39 ft. 4 in.; length, 29 ft. 1⅝ in.; height, 13 ft. 3¾ in.; wing area, 252.952 sq. ft.*

KAWANISHI N1K2-J SHIDEN-KAI (GEORGE 21)   JAPAN

Although the N1K1-J Shiden 11 had exceeded the most sanguine expectations it suffered several serious faults stemming from its hurried development, these sometimes rendering a unit impotent before it had lost an aircraft in combat. The wheel brakes were so bad that the Shiden 11 was often landed on rough ground alongside a runway in order to reduce the length of the landing run. To rectify these and other failings a complete redesign of the fighter was undertaken by Kawanishi in mid-1943—the result, the Shiden-Kai, was undoubtedly the finest J.N.A.F. production fighter of the war.

The Shiden-Kai was redesigned largely with an eye to simplification. Excluding nuts and bolts, only 43,000 parts were employed as compared to the 66,000 of the original Shiden, and pre-formed sheet was extensively used. Although the Homare 21 was still extremely unreliable, it was retained for the redesigned

fighter owing to its immediate availability. Like its predecessor, the Shiden-Kai was ordered into production off the drawing board, and work proceeded rapidly as a result of the assignment of personnel released from the N1K1-J and the Kawanishi J6K1 Jimpu (development of which had been abandoned) to the Shiden-Kai design staff.

On December 31, 1943, the prototype N1K2-J Shiden-Kai was flown for the first time and immediately accepted by the J.N.A.F. as the Shiden 21. A further seven prototypes were completed by June 1944, but three months before this the Naruo plant had begun to tool up for the quantity production of the Shiden-Kai, and once again, as with the original Shiden, test results were applied directly to production aircraft on the assembly lines, resulting in confusion and delay. The situation was worsened by a series of teething troubles which proved difficult to eliminate. These

A standard N1K2-J fighter. This employed 23,000 less parts than original Shiden.

7

substantially delayed the production programme, and bombing by B-29 Superfortresses led to shortages of Homare engines, steel forgings, aluminium extrusions, landing gear assemblies, etc. Thus, only sixty Shiden-Kai fighters were produced by the Naruo plant between July and the end of 1944, and only 294 subsequently. Production did not start at Himeji until March 1945, and only forty-four were completed by that factory. Construction of the N1K2-J was also assigned to Mitsubishi's 7th airframe plant (where nine were completed between March and August 1945), to the Ettoku plant of Aichi (where only one was completed in July 1945), to the Shinonoi plant of Showa (one being completed in August 1945), and to the Naval Air Arsenals at Hiro (one completed), Omura (ten completed), and Atsugi (none completed). Actual

production by all manufacturers up to the end of the war totalled only 428 machines.

Externally, the Shiden 21 differed appreciably from the Shiden 11. A low-wing supplanted the mid-wing, enabling the complex system of double retraction for the mainwheel legs to be eliminated; the fuselage was lengthened substantially and refined; the contours of the engine cowling were improved, and the vertical tail surfaces were entirely redesigned. The sum total of these changes was, in the hands of a competent pilot, perhaps the best all-round fighter operational in the Pacific. On one occasion, a Shiden 21 flown by Flight Warrant Officer Kinsuke Muto succeeded in destroying four out of twelve Grumman Hellcats before they broke off the combat and returned to their carrier.

A small number of machines were completed

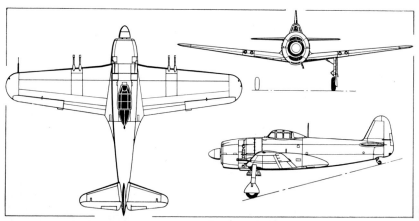

This experimental model of the Shiden-Kai featured a cleaner, redesigned engine cowling.

as N1K2-K Shiden-Rensen two-seat dual-control trainers, but one of the first major revisions of the single-seat Shiden-Kai was the N1K3-J Shiden 31 which had the Homare 21 moved forward six inches to improve the c.g. position, and the standard wing-mounted armament of four 20-mm. guns supplemented by twin 13.2-mm. Type 3 machine guns in the forward fuselage decking. The shipboard N1K3-A Shiden 41 was also proposed, but neither model was built. Work on the N1K4-J powered by the 2,000 h.p. NK9H-S Homare 23 with low-pressure fuel-injection system began late in 1944, and three experimental prototypes were completed under the designation Shiden 32. A shipboard variant of this development, the N1K4-A, was also built and tested in prototype form, but before production could begin this version was abandoned owing to the complete destruction of Japan's carrier forces. In an attempt to improve the effectiveness of the Shiden as a Superfortress interceptor, a 2,200 h.p. Mitsubishi MK9A (Ha.43/11) engine was to have been installed in the N1K5-J, but the sole prototype was destroyed during a Superfortress attack on Himeji in June 1945.

Type: *Single-seat Interceptor and Fighter-bomber.* **Power Plant:** *One 1,990 h.p. Nakajima NK9H Homare 21 eighteen-cylinder radial air-cooled engine.* **Armament:** *Four 20-mm. Type 99 Model 2 cannon plus two 550-lb. bombs.* **Performance:** *Maximum speed, 369 m.p.h. at 18,370 ft., 359 m.p.h. at 9,840 ft.; cruising speed, 230 m.p.h. at 9,840 ft.; normal range, 1,066 mls., (with 88 Imp. gal. drop tank) 1,450 mls.; time to 19,685 ft., 7 min. 22 sec.; service ceiling, 35,300 ft.* **Weights:** *Empty, 5,858 lb.; loaded, 9,039 lb.* **Dimensions:** *Span, 39 ft. 4 in.; length, 30 ft. 8 in.; height, 13 ft. 0 in.; wing area, 252.952 sq. ft.*

KAWANISHI P1Y2-S KYOKKO (FRANCES 26)   JAPAN

The P1Y2-S Kyokko (Aurora) night fighter

(*Above*) *A P1Y1-S Kyokko night fighter converted from a P1Y1 Ginga bomber. This aircraft retained the dorsal turret with twin 20-mm. cannon featured by some Ginga bombers but carried no radar.*

was one of the several types of bomber hastily converted for nocturnal interception duties as Japan was faced with an ever-growing threat of large-scale night attacks on her industrial centres. The Kyokko was derived from the Y-20 15-*Shi* twin-engined land-based bomber designed by the Dai-ichi Kaigun Gijitsucho (1st Naval Air Technical Arsenal) at Yokosuka, and which, adopted as the P1Y1 Ginga (Milky Way) was built in quantity from 1943 onwards by the Nakajima Hikoki K.K.

The Ginga was an exceptionally fine design, but it demanded an extremely high standard of manufacturing skill and, in consequence, underwent a number of revisions aimed at simplifying manufacture. The 1,820 h.p. Nakajima Homare 11 eighteen-cylinder radials proved troublesome, and the oil system of the Ginga was particularly complex and resulted in serious field maintenance problems. Consequently, when Kawanishi were awarded a production contract for a night-fighter version

(*Above and below*) *A standard P1Y2-S Kyokko with A.I. radar antennae. Only ninety-seven were built.*

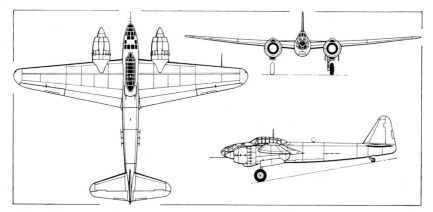

of the Ginga, a considerable amount of re-design was undertaken.

Initially, Kawanishi adopted the 1,850 h.p. Mitsubishi Kasei 25 fourteen-cylinder radial in order to overcome the difficulties experienced with the Homare, and with these engines two production versions were proposed, the P1Y2 Ginga bomber and the P1Y2-S Kyokko night fighter. The latter was given priority in view of the urgent need for night fighters, and the prototype Kyokko was completed in June 1944, production being initiated as the P1Y2-S Night Fighter, Model 26. The Kyokko was fitted with primitive A.I. radar and an arma-ment of three 20-mm. cannon, two of these fixed amidships at an oblique angle to fire forward and upward and one being mounted flexibly in the rear cockpit. Only ninety-seven P1Y2-S Kyokko night fighters were completed, and it was intended to introduce these as Superfortress interceptors, but they were still

undergoing service trials when Japan capitu-lated. A small number of Nakajima-built P1Y1-S night fighters were also produced as conversions of standard P1Y1 bombers, and some of these mounted twin 20-mm. cannon in a manually-operated dorsal turret. A projected version was the P1Y3-S with 1,990 h.p. Homare engines.

Type: *Three-seat Night Fighter.* **Power Plants:** *Two 1,850 h.p. Mitsubishi Kasei 25 fourteen-cylinder radial air-cooled engines.* **Armament:** *Three 20-mm. Type 99 cannon.* **Performance:** *Maximum speed, 325 m.p.h. at 17,720 ft.; cruising speed, 230 m.p.h. at 13,120 ft.; time to 16,400 ft., 9 min. 23 sec.; service ceiling, 31,365 ft.* **Weights:** *Empty, 17,196 lb.; normal loaded, 23,148 lb.; maximum, 29,762 lb.* **Dimensions:** *Span, 65 ft. 7½ in.; length, 49 ft. 2½ in.; height, 14 ft. 1¼ in.; wing area, 592.014 sq. ft.*

KAWASAKI KI.45 TORYU (NICK)   JAPAN

During the 'thirties, the J.A.A.F. watched with interest the development of heavy twin-engined fighters in Germany and the U.S.A.,

and, in March 1937, concluded that such a strategic fighter could be of value for long-range operations over the Pacific. Accordingly, Kawasaki Kokuki Kogyo K.K. was instructed to proceed with a preliminary design study for a twin-engined long-range escort fighter, the project being assigned the designation Ki.38. A mock-up was completed in October 1937, but so many changes were demanded by the J.A.A.F. that a complete redesign was called for, and, in December, this extensively modified project became the Ki.45, later to be dubbed Toryu (Dragon Killer).

The chosen power plant for the Ki.45 was the Ha.20B radial air-cooled engine which,

(Left) An early production Ki.45-KAI and (below) a Ki.45-KAI of the Akeno Fighter Training School.

Standard production Ki.45-KAIa fighter and (below) a Ki.45-KAIa of the 10th Air Division.

still under development, was expected to have a maximum rating of 820 h.p. at 11,480 ft. By the time the first Toryu was delivered in January 1939, however, the Ha.20B was giving appreciably less power than that anticipated. Another problem which arose during initial flight trials was provided by the undercarriage, the manual retraction system failing to function efficiently. The latter fault was rectified by the provision of an electrically-actuated retraction mechanism, but all attempts to boost the output of the Ha.20B failed. Kawasaki even attempted the redesign of the engine themselves and, at one time, contemplated the use of contra-rotating airscrews, but in April 1940, after six prototypes had been tested, the J.A.A.F. decided to discontinue its support for the Ha.20B and, instead, adopt the Ha.25

A Ki.45-KAIc of the 53rd Fighter Squadron based at Matsudo, near Tokyo, in the Spring of 1945.

rated at 1,000 h.p. for take-off and 980 h.p. at 9,840 ft., three of the prototypes being re-engined under the designation Ki.45-I.

The first Ki.45-I was flown in July 1940, but during the flight a violent engine stall resulted when the pilot opened the cowling flaps, and the prototype suffered considerable damage in the emergency landing that followed. After modifications and repairs, trials were resumed in August, and a further five prototypes were completed with Ha.25 engines.

When the fighter eventually entered production in September 1941 at Kawasaki's Gifu plant as the Ki.45-KAI Toryu Type 2 Heavy Fighter, the fuselage length and wing span had both been increased. The Ki.45-KAI carried a forward-firing armament of one 20-mm. cannon and two 12.7-mm. machine guns, and the observer was provided with a single 7.92-mm. machine gun. In addition, two 550-lb. bombs could be carried on underwing racks between the engine nacelles and fuselage. By the late summer of 1942, when Kawasaki's Akashi factory joined the Toryu production programme, the 1,080 h.p. Ha.102 engine, a direct development of the Ha.25, and various improvements dictated by operational experience resulted in the Ki.45-KAIa (Type 2 Heavy Fighter, Model A). Externally, the Ki.45-KAIa differed little from the initial production model, apart from a more pointed nose, but the Ki.45-KAIb (Model B) introduced a 37-mm. cannon which, mounted ventrally, was loaded by the observer. A single forward-firing 12.7-mm. gun was retained for aiming purposes. Various alternative combinations of forward-firing guns were introduced as production proceeded. In some aircraft the single 12.7-mm. gun was supplanted by a 20-mm. cannon, while other machines had no rear-firing 7.92-mm. gun but carried two forward-firing 20-mm. cannon in addition to the 37-mm. weapon. Experimental installations included a combination of two 37-mm. and two 12.7-mm. weapons, while one variant was fitted with a single 75-mm. cannon for anti-shipping duties.

The Ki.45-KAIc and KAId embodied a number of internal refinements, and could be fitted with five combinations of cannon of various calibres and machine guns. Many of these were adapted for the night-fighting role with two fixed 12.7-mm. machine guns installed aft of the pilot and firing forward and upward at an angle of 30°. This mounting, which was devised by Colonel Yasuna Kozono of the Japanese Navy's 251st Air Corps, and introduced on the Toryu in 1944, was extremely successful, and was adopted by the Luftwaffe by whom it was known as "Schräge Musik". Some machines were fitted with a small searchlight in the nose, and the normal armament of late production Ki.45-KAIc Toryu night fighters comprised a single forward firing 37-mm. cannon and two obliquely-mounted 20-mm. cannon aft of the pilot. A few retained the flexible 7.92-mm. gun in the observer's cockpit and some even carried a 20-mm. cannon in this position. The Toryu was one of the most successful of Japanese night fighters, and served with the J.A.A.F.'s 10th Division in the defence of the Tokyo area.

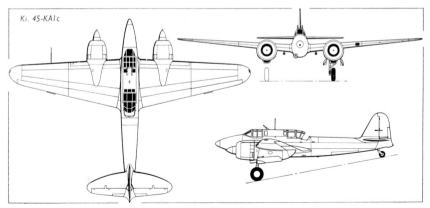

Ki. 45-KAIc

(*Above and below*) *The Ki.45-KAIc night fighter with obliquely-mounted 20-mm. cannon aft of pilot.*

Work on a more powerful Toryu, the Ki.45-II with 1,500 h.p. Ha.112-II radials, began in August 1942, but this was later converted as a single-seater under the designation Ki.96. Kawasaki's Gifu and Akashi plants produced 1,687 Toryu fighters plus 11 prototypes, and the type was employed extensively throughout the J.A.A.F.'s sphere of operations. When B-29 Superfortresses bombed Japan from Chinese bases for the first time on June 15, 1944, they were intercepted by a force of eight Toryu fighters which subsequently claimed to have destroyed seven of the bombers and probably three more. The Toryu was encountered over Rangoon, in Sumatra and Manchuria, and in New Guinea, on May 27, 1944, four Toryus initiated the pattern for subsequent suicide attacks when they attacked Allied vessels steaming up the northern coastline.

The following specification relates to the late production Ki.45-KAIc night fighter.

Type: Two-seat Night Fighter. **Power Plants:** *Two 1,080 h.p. Mitsubishi Ha.102 Type 1 fourteen-cylinder radial air-cooled engines.* **Armament:** *One 37-mm. Ho-203 cannon and two obliquely-mounted 20-mm. Type 2 cannon.* **Performance:** *Maximum speed, 340 m.p.h. at 22,965 ft., 335 m.p.h. at 19,685 ft.; cruising speed, 236 m.p.h.; normal range, 746 mls.; maximum range, 932 mls.; time to 16,400 ft., 7 min.; service ceiling, 32,810 ft.* **Weights:** *Empty, 8,818 lb.; loaded, 12,125 lb.* **Dimensions:** *Span, 49 ft. 5¼ in.; length, 36 ft. 1 in.; height, 12 ft. 1¾ in.; wing area, 344.445 sq. ft.*

The early months of the war in Europe led the J.A.A.F. to consider the possible need for heavier fighters with liquid-cooled engines comparable with the latest European designs. The Kawasaki Kokuki Kogyo K.K. had already acquired a manufacturing licence for the Daimler-Benz series of liquid-cooled inline engines, and several examples of the DB 601A had been shipped to Japan. This power plant was selected for a new cannon-armed heavy fighter, the Ki.60, for which a development contract was placed with Kawasaki in February 1940. Like the Mitsubishi M-20 to be ordered by the J.N.A.F. shortly afterwards as a part of the 14-*Shi* programme, the Ki.60 denoted a complete reversal of previous Japanese fighter practice in that speed and climb rate took the place of manoeuvrability as primary requirements.

The Ki.60 was a relatively clean, all-metal stressed-skin monoplane carrying what was, by Japanese standards appertaining at the time, a heavy armament. This was to have comprised two 20-mm. Mauser MG 151

cannon and two 12.7-mm. machine guns or four 12.7-mm. machine guns. The first of three Ki.60 prototypes was flown in March 1941, this aircraft possessing a wing area of 171.146 sq. ft. Owing to its high wing loading

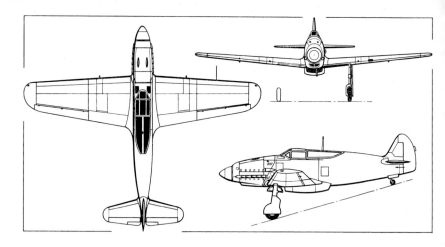

by comparison with other J.A.A.F. fighters and, consequently, inferior take-off and landing performance, flight test reports were unfavourable. The second and third prototypes had modified wings of 174.376 sq. ft. gross area but showed little improvement over the first machine, and although design estimates had indicated a maximum speed of 375 m.p.h., only 354 m.p.h. was attained by the first prototype during tests, while the second attained only 348 m.p.h.

The disappointing performance of the Ki.60 and the fact that J.A.A.F. pilots were demanding greater manoeuvrability than was offered by this fighter, combined with the J.A.A.F.'s lack of serious plans for the introduction of heavy fighters resulted, at the end of 1941,

in the decision to abandon the Ki.60 in favour of the Ki.61 which had been developed in parallel by Kawasaki.

Type: *Single-seat Interceptor Fighter.* **Power Plant:** *One 1,100 h.p. Daimler-Benz DB 601A twelve-cylinder inverted-Vee liquid-cooled engine.* **Armament:** *Two 20-mm. Mauser MG 151 cannon and two 12.7-mm. Type 1 machine guns or four 12.7-mm. Type 1 machine guns.* **Performance:** *Maximum speed, 348 m.p.h. at 16,400 ft.; time to 16,400 ft., 8 min.; service ceiling, 32,810 ft.* **Weights:** *Empty, 4,740 lb.; normal loaded, 6,063 lb.* **Dimensions:** *Span, 34 ft. 5½ in.; length, 27 ft. 9½ in.; height, 9 ft. 10 in.; wing area, 174.376 sq. ft.*

KAWASAKI KI.61 HIEN (TONY)

The only Japanese fighter powered by a liquid-cooled engine to see operational service, the Ki.61 Hien (Swallow) was mistakenly believed to be a licence-built version of the Messerschmitt Bf 109 when it was first encountered by the Allies over New Guinea in April 1943. In fact, the design of the Hien was influenced in no way by the Messerschmitt fighter, the first prototype having flown six months before the arrival in Japan of an example of the Bf 109 from Germany.

Design and construction of the Ki.61 was ordered in February 1940, and proceeded in parallel with the heavier Ki.60. While prototype construction was in progress, Kawasaki's Akashi plant was actively engaged in adapting the Daimler-Benz DB 601A for Japanese production techniques. Lighter in weight than

the DB 601A the Japanese version of this power plant was designated Ha.40 and, rated at 1,175 h.p. for take-off, was selected for installation in the Ki.61, the first of twelve prototypes of which was completed and flown in December 1941. The prototypes were exhaustively tested in mock-combat with the Bf 109E and captured examples of the Curtiss P-40E, and were generally considered by the Japanese to be superior to both German and American fighters in nearly all respects.

The fighter entered production as the Ki.61-I Hien Type 3 Fighter, Model 1, the first machine being delivered to the J.A.A.F. by the Kagamigahara plant in August 1942, powered by the production version of the Ha.40 engine, the (Ha.60/22) Type 2. Thirty-four Hien fighters were completed in 1942, after which

An early production Ki.61-I Hien Type 3 Fighter Model 1 with two wing-mounted 12.7-mm. guns.

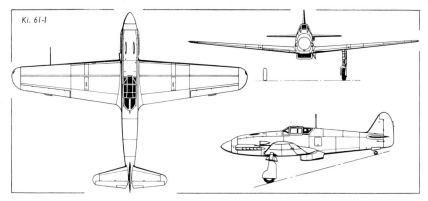

Ki. 61-I

production tempo increased rapidly, attaining a monthly output of 100 machines in November 1943, and reaching a peak at 254 machines monthly in July 1944. Introduced over New Guinea in April 1943, the Hien rapidly appeared in every theatre of operations in

A Ki.61-I Hien Type 3 Fighter Model 1.

which the J.A.A.F. participated, being encountered over Rabaul in New Britain, the Admiralty Islands, the Chinese mainland, and later in the defence of Manila, the Leyte peninsula in the Philippines, and the Japanese home islands.

The initial production model carried two 7.7-mm. machine guns in the fuselage and two 12.7-mm. guns in the wings, but in August 1943 the 12.7-mm. guns were supplanted by imported 20-mm. Mauser MG 151, the fighter being known as the Ki.61-Ia (Model 1A) with this modification. As the tide of war turned against Germany, however, shipment of the Mauser cannon and their ammunition to Japan was curtailed. The Japanese had foreseen this possibility and were developing a comparable cannon of indigenous design, the 20-mm. Ho-5, but this was not available in quantity when the supply of MG 151s dried up (400 Hien fighters having received the German guns) and, as an interim measure, production continued with the Ki.61-Ib which had an armament of four 12.7-mm. machine guns.

In service, the Hien had proved capable of holding its own against the heavier American fighters. It could be pushed over in a 45° dive with remarkable rapidity and its diving characteristics were excellent. Manoeuvrability was inferior to that of the earlier Ki.43 Hayabusa, but the Hien was faster, and the provision of self-sealing fuel tanks and armour protection for the pilot fostered the aggressive employment of the fighter. The Hien was not an easy aircraft to service under operational conditions, however, and defects in the Ha.40 engine became ever-increasing sources of trouble. Main-bearing failures and oil-system faults were the principal problems. Considerable attention was given to the problems of field maintenance, and in January 1944 tests began with the Ki.61-Ic (Model 1C), the first production variant to receive the domestically-manufactured 20-mm. Ho-5 cannon, two of which were mounted in the wings. A number of improvements to the controls were also made,

A Ki.61-Ia Hien with wing-mounted 20-mm. Mauser MG 151 cannon. Only 400 aircraft received these guns.

and a detachable rear fuselage was introduced to simplify maintenance. The Ki.61-Ic was succeeded in production by the Ki.61-Id in which 30-mm. cannon supplanted the wing-mounted 20-mm. guns. By the spring of 1944 production of the Hien was falling owing to shortages of Ha.40 engines (no solution having been found for the bearing failures), and deliveries of the Ki.61-I finally terminated in January 1945 with the 2,654th machine.

Development of a more powerful variant of the Hien, the Ki.61-II (Model 2) had begun in September 1942. Intended to take a new Kawasaki power plant, the Ha.140 rated at 1,500 h.p. for take-off, the Ki.61-II featured a larger wing and a redesigned cockpit canopy to improve pilot visibility. The first machine was completed in August 1943, but only eight aircraft had been completed by January 1944 owing to teething troubles suffered by the new

(Above) A standard Ki.61-*I* Hien and *(below)* Hien *fighters of the Akeno Fighter Training School.*

engine and structural weaknesses that had manifested themselves during flight trials. The latter rendered a complete structural redesign necessary, resulting in the Ki.61-II-KAI. Whereas the wing of the Ki.61-II had an area of 237.6 sq. ft., the Ki.61-II-KAI reverted to the 215.278 sq. ft. wing of the Ki.61-I, embodied a stronger airframe and featured enlarged and redesigned vertical tail surfaces to compensate for the longer engine. The first Ki.61-II-KAI was completed in April 1944, and this version of the Hien entered production at Kagamigahara as the Ki.61-IIa (Type 3 Fighter, Model 2A) armed with two 12.7-mm. and two 20-mm. guns, and as the Ki.61-IIb with four 20-mm. cannon.

The Ha.140 rapidly proved itself to be a totally unreliable engine, and only thirty Ki.61-IIa and IIb Hien fighters had been produced in the spring of 1944 when deliveries of the Ha.140 dried up. Limited production was resumed in August 1944 and continued at a low rate, but only ninety-nine fighters were completed with the Ha.140 by January 19, 1945 when a B-29 raid brought production of the engine to an end. Of the Ki.61-IIa and IIb fighters completed, about one-third were destroyed in air raids, and the remainder were immediately assigned to duty as interceptors. Variations in the rated power of the Ha.140 engine owing to poor quality workmanship kept performance well below that anticipated, but

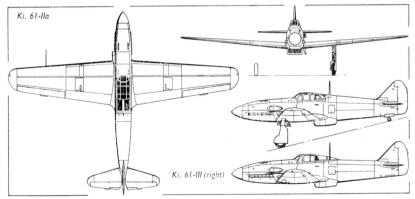

Ki. 61-IIa

Ki. 61-III (right)

A Ki.61-Ib Hien captured in China. The Ki.61-Ib carried four wing-mounted 12.7-mm. Type 1 guns.

A Ki.61-IIa Type 3 Fighter Model 2A.

the fighter could maintain combat formation at altitudes as great as 33,000 ft., and climb rate was good.

The final development of the Hien to retain the liquid-cooled engine was the Ki.61-III (Model 3) which featured a cut-down rear fuselage and all-round-vision cockpit canopy. This model failed to attain production, however, as production of the Hien was totally suspended in favour of the Ki.100.

The specification relates to the Ki.61-Ic, figures in parentheses referring to the -IIb.

Type: *Single-seat Interceptor Fighter and Fighter-bomber.* **Power Plant:** *One 1,175 (1,500) h.p. Kawasaki Ha.40 (Ha.140) Type 2 twelve-cylinder inverted-Vee liquid-cooled engine.* **Armament:** *Two 20-mm. Ho-5 cannon and two 12.7-mm. Type 1 machine guns plus two 550-lb. bombs.* **Performance:** *Maximum speed, 348 (373) m.p.h. at 16,400 (19,685) ft., 302 m.p.h. at sea level; maximum range, 1,185 (746) mls.; cruising speed, 215 m.p.h. at 1,500 ft.; time to 16,400 ft., 7 (6.5) min.; service ceiling, 32,800 (36,090) ft.* **Weights:** *Empty, 5,798 (6,261) lb.; loaded, 7,650 (8,333) lb.* **Dimensions:** *Span, 39 ft. 4 in.; length, 29 ft. 4 in. (30 ft. 0¼ in.); height, 12 ft. 1¾ in. (11 ft. 5 in.); wing area, 215.278 sq. ft.*

KAWASAKI KI.64 (ROB)   JAPAN

The Ki.64 experimental heavy fighter for the J.A.A.F. was one of the most advanced and unorthodox warplanes developed by the Japanese aircraft industry during the war years. Conceived in 1939, the Ki.64 combined tandem-mounted engines and contra-rotating airscrews with a system of surface evaporation cooling. The Kawasaki Ha.201 twenty-four cylinder inline engine actually comprised two Ha.40s (Japanese versions of the Daimler-Benz DB 601A) mounted fore and aft of the pilot's cockpit, and was cooled by steam vapour which was led to condensers in the wings. The surface evaporation cooling system was tested on a Ki.61 Hien (Swallow) at Kawasaki's Akashi plant during the summer of 1943,

and the experimental machine attained a maximum speed 25 m.p.h. higher than that of the standard Hien.

Although preliminary studies for the Ki.64 had been made in 1939, more pressing commitments necessitated the shelving of the project until October 1940 when detail design began. The prototype was completed in December 1943, and flight trials began before the end of the month. Although the first four flights were relatively successful, during the fifth flight a fire started in the rear component of the power plant as the result of an oil lead fracturing, necessitating a forced landing. The only serious damage was suffered by the undercarriage; however, this delayed the test

The sole prototype Ki.64 experimental fighter taking-off on its initial flight in December 1943.

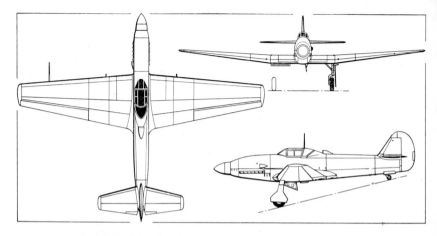

programme. The initial flight trials had indicated the need for modifications to the contra-rotating airscrews. The forward airscrew was of controllable-pitch type and the rear airscrew was a fixed-pitch unit. It was decided to replace this unsatisfactory arrangement with an electric constant-speed contra-prop with which the fighter prototype was to have been redesignated Ki.64-KAI. The development of a suitable contra-prop took appreciably longer than had been anticipated, however, and as by this time the war situation had become extremely critical for Japan, it was decided to suspend further work on the Ki.64 in favour of research offering the prospect of more immediate results.

The Kawasaki Ha.201 engine installed in the sole prototype Ki.64 was rated at 2,350 h.p. for take-off and 2,200 h.p. at 12,795 ft., but it was

hoped to boost output to 2,800 h.p. with which a maximum speed of the order of 500 m.p.h. was anticipated. The proposed armament of the Ki.64 was four 20-mm. cannon, and it was proposed to protract endurance by shutting down one of the two components of the Ha.201 engine.

Type: *Single-seat Interceptor Fighter.* **Power Plant:** *One 2,350 h.p. Kawasaki Ha.201 twenty-four-cylinder inverted-Vee engine.* **Armament** (*Proposed*): *Four 20-mm. Type Ho-5 cannon.* **Performance:** *Maximum speed, 429 m.p.h. at 16,400 ft.; normal range, 620 mls.; time to 16,400 ft., 5 min. 30 sec.; service ceiling, 39,370 ft.* **Weights:** *Empty, 8,929 lb.; loaded, 11,244 lb.* **Dimensions:** *Span, 44 ft. 3½ in.; length, 36 ft. 2¼ in.; height, 10 ft. 5¼ in.; wing area, 301.389 sq. ft.*

KAWASAKI KI.96   JAPAN

The success achieved by the J.A.A.F. with the Ki. 45 Toryu (Dragon Killer) prompted Kawasaki to consider a refined, more powerful heavy fighter based broadly on the design of the Toryu. Conceived as a two-seat multi-purpose fighter with a heavy forward-firing armament and two Mitsubishi Ha.112-II fourteen-cylinder radials, the project was assigned the designation Ki.96, and the construction of three prototypes started in August 1942.

In December 1942, the J.A.A.F., having become interested in the possibilities of the heavy single-seat fighter, instructed Kawasaki to complete the Ki.96 as a single-seater. The first prototype, which was completed in September 1943, had the second cockpit faired over, but the second and third prototypes, which had been built as single-seaters from the outset, had redesigned, all-round-vision canopies. The Ki.96 was a low mid-wing monoplane of all-metal construction with an oval-section flush-riveted stressed-skin fuselage and two-spar wing. Performance exceeded design estimates, a maximum speed of 373

(Above, right, and below) The third prototype Ki.96 single-seat heavy fighter tested in 1944.

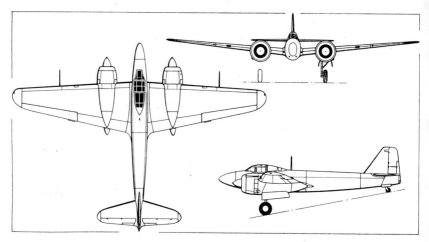

m.p.h. being attained at 19,685 feet, but despite earlier interest in the twin-engined single-seat fighter concept, the J.A.A.F. had not formulated any definite policy for the use of such machines, and it was decided to revert to the original two-seat configuration. In consequence, further development of the Ki.96 was abandoned, the wings, tail assembly and engines being adapted for use by the two-seat Ki.102 heavy attack fighter.

The first prototype Ki.96 completed as a single-seater with second cockpit faired over.

Type: *Single-seat Heavy Interceptor and Attack Fighter.* **Power Plants:** *Two 1,500 h.p. Mitsubishi Ha.112-II fourteen-cylinder radial air-cooled engines.* **Armament:** *One 37-mm. Ho-203 cannon and two 20-mm. Ho-5 cannon.* **Performance:** *Maximum speed, 373 m.p.h. at 19,685 ft.; normal range (on internal fuel), 994 mls.; time to 16,400 ft., 6 min.; service ceiling, 37,730 ft.* **Weights:** *Empty, 10,031 lb.; loaded, 13,228 lb.* **Dimensions:** *Span, 51 ft. 1 in.; length, 37 ft. 6¾ in.; height, 12 ft. 1⅝ in.; wing area, 365.973 sq. ft.*

KAWASAKI KI.100

In March 1945 Allied aircraft operating over the Japanese home islands began to encounter an exceptionally potent interceptor fighter which appeared in none of the Allied recognition manuals. Possessing a definite ascendancy over the Grumman F6F Hellcat and the equal of the formidable P-51D Mustang, the new J.A.A.F. fighter displayed a radical advance in combat potential over its predecessors—an advance which came as much as a surprise to its manufacturers as to the Allies, who little expected to meet a new type of fighter at that late stage of the war. But the new fighter, the Kawasaki Ki.100-la Type 5 Fighter, Model 1A, was *not* an entirely new machine. It was an improvisation forced upon the J.A.A.F. by mounting stocks of Ki.61-II Hien airframes and diminishing supplies of Kawasaki Ha.140 liquid-cooled engines.

By the end of 1944 some 270 Ki.61-II airframes were standing at Kawasaki factories with little likelihood of ever receiving Ha.140 engines, deliveries of which had dropped to a mere trickle. The fighters were required urgently by the J.A.A.F., and there was no alternative but to install a different engine. However, the only engine offering a suitable output was the Mitsubishi Ha.112-II, a large-diameter radial which appeared totally unsuited for marriage to an airframe designed for a slim liquid-cooled engine. Nevertheless, Kawasaki engineers undertook the conversion, the first of three Ki.61-II airframes fitted with the Ha.112-II flying on February 1, 1945. The adaptation immediately proved to be far more successful than the most sanguine expectations could have foreseen, and as the Ki.100-Ia Type 5 Fighter, Model 1A, the

Ki.100-Ia Type 5 Model 1A fighters which employed Ki.61-II airframes.

29

A Ki.100-Ib fighter of the J.A.A.F.'s 5th Fighter Squadron which operated in defence of the home islands.

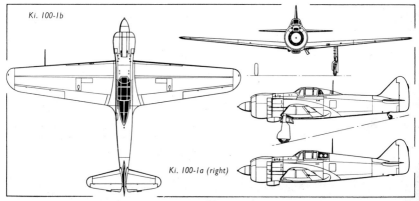

Ki. 100-Ib

Ki. 100-Ia (right)

existing stock of Ki.61-II airframes was quickly converted to take the radial engine, thirty-six being delivered in March, eighty-nine in April, and one hundred and thirty-one in May.

With the completion of these conversions, the fighter was built from the ground up as the Ki.100-Ib, this differing from the original model solely in having an all-round-vision hood similar to that developed for the Ki.61-III. Ninety-nine Ki.100-Ib fighters had left the Kagamigahara plant by the end of June when production was brought to a sudden standstill by aerial attacks. In March 1945, an attempt to improve the altitude potentiality of the basic design resulted in the start of work on the Ki.100-II with an Ha.112-IIru engine. This engine was fitted with an Ru.102 turbo-supercharger and a methanol/water injection system to boost output for short bursts. The turbo-supercharger was placed below the engine and displaced some of the fuel system components, but space limitations prohibited the installation of an aftercooler and its associated ducting, and air was ducted directly from the compressor to the carburettor. The Ki.100-II flew within six weeks of development being initiated, the second within eight

(Right and below) The Ki.100-Ib Type 5, one of the most successful improvisations of the war.

(Above and left) The Ki.100-Ib Type 5.

weeks and the third within ten weeks. The lack of an intercooler limited the high-altitude performance of the Ki.100-II, and the turbo-supercharger added 600 lb. to its weight, reducing maximum speed by approximately 15 m.p.h. at 10,000 ft. However the boosted power at 30,000 ft. gave the Ki.100-II a 30 m.p.h. speed advantage over the initial model at this altitude, although both types possessed the same service ceiling.

Ki.100 fighters were primarily assigned to the defence of the home islands, operating from Chofu and Yokkaichi from the spring of 1945.

Type: *Single-seat Interceptor Fighter and Fighter-bomber.* **Power Plant:** *One 1,500 h.p. Mitsubishi Ha.112-II Type 4 fourteen-cylinder radial air-cooled engine.* **Armament:** *Two 20-mm. Ho-5 cannon and two 12.7-mm. Type 103 machine guns.* **Performance:** *Maximum speed, 367 m.p.h. at 32,800 ft.; cruising speed, 217 m.p.h.; range, 1,243 mls.; time to 16,400 ft., 6 min. 42 sec.; service ceiling, 35,000 ft.* **Weights:** *Empty, 5,952 lb.; loaded, 8,091 lb.* **Dimensions:** *Span, 39 ft. 4¼ in.; length, 28 ft. 11 in.; height, 12 ft. 3¾ in.; wing area, 215.278 sq. ft.*

KAWASAKI KI.102 (RANDY)   JAPAN

Stemming from the Ki.96 single-seat heavy fighter and, in its original form, retaining the wings, tail assembly and engines of the earlier design, the Ki.102 was a heavy two-seat attack fighter intended primarily for close-support missions. Design work was begun in August 1943, and the first of three prototypes was completed in March 1944. The prototypes were closely followed by twenty pre-production Ki.102b's for service trials, and in October 1944 quantity production started as the Type 4 Assault Fighter.

Forward-firing armament comprised one 57-mm. and two 20-mm. cannon, and during a trial flight at Tachikawa, one of the pre-production Ki.102b aircraft had an opportunity to demonstrate the potency of its large-calibre cannon when it shot an engine off a passing B-29 Superfortress with one shell. In addition to the forward-firing armament, a 1,100-lb. bomb load could be carried, and the observer

was provided with a 12.7-mm. machine gun.

Prior to the delivery of the first pre-production Ki.102b consideration had been given to the adaptation of the basic design as a high-altitude interceptor under the designation Ki.102a with turbo-supercharged Ha.112-IIru engines affording 1,370 h.p. at 22,965 ft. (the standard Ha.112-II giving this power at 6,560 ft.). This variant was designated Ki.102a, and six pre-production Ki.102b heavy fighters were modified as interceptors to serve as prototypes. The first Ki.102a was tested in June 1944, and in November the highest priority was given to the quantity production of the fighter. Armament comprised one 37-mm. and two 20-mm. cannon, but unexpected difficulties with the turbo-superchargers delayed production, and only fifteen Ki.102a interceptors had been delivered to the J.A.A.F. by the end of the war.

With the intensification of night attacks on

A Ki.102b two-seat attack fighter seen during operational evaluation with the J.A.A.F.

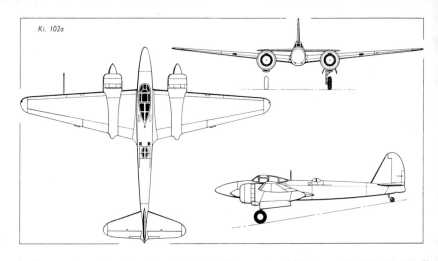

Ki. 102a

the Japanese home islands at the end of 1944, the basic design was modified for the night-fighting role as the Ki.102c. The fuselage was lengthened, the wing span and area were increased, the tail surfaces were redesigned, primitive interception radar was placed above the fuselage, and two 20-mm. cannon were mounted to fire obliquely upwards in the rear fuselage. Only two Ki.102c night fighters were completed, production being hampered by constant air attacks by B-29 Superfortresses.

The following specification relates to the Ki.102b, figures in parentheses referring specifically to the Ki.102c.

Type: *Two-seat Attack (Night) Fighter.* **Power Plants:** *Two 1,500 h.p. Mitsubishi Ha.112-II (-IIru) fourteen-cylinder radial air-cooled engines.* **Armament:** *One 57-mm. Ho-401 cannon, two 20-mm. Ho-5 cannon and one 12.7-mm. Ho-103 machine gun plus a 1,100-lb. bomb load (two forward-firing 30-mm. cannon and two obliquely-mounted 20-mm. cannon).* **Performance:** *Maximum speed, 360 (373) m.p.h. at 19,685 (32,810) ft.; range, 1,243 (839) mls.; time to 16,400 ft., 6 min. 54 sec., to 32,800 ft., 18 min.; service ceiling, 36,090 (32,810) ft.* **Weights:** *Empty, 10,913 (11,464) lb.; loaded, 16,094 (16,755) lb.* **Dimensions:** *Span, 50 ft. 1 in. (56 ft. 7⅛ in.); length, 37 ft. 6¾ in. (42 ft. 9¾ in.); height, 12 ft. 1⅞ in. (12 ft. 1⅞ in.); wing area, 365.973 (430.556) sq. ft.*

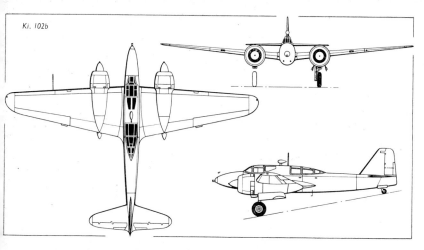

Ki. 102b

Testing of the Ki.102b began in June 1944, and production had high priority.

35

KAWASAKI KI.108   JAPAN

Final development of the series of twin-engined fighters stemming from the Ki.45 Toryu was the Ki.108 conceived as a pressurised high-altitude heavy interceptor. In April 1943, Kawasaki received a J.A.A.F. directive for the development of an experimental fighter for operation at extreme altitudes, and to simplify the project, it was decided to adapt the basic design of the two-seat Ki.102, upon which work had just commenced, to meet the new requirement.

While work proceeded on the Ki.102 prototypes, a pressure cabin was developed for installation in the single-seat high-altitude version which had been allocated the designation Ki.108. This cabin gave the equivalent pressure of 9,800 ft. at an altitude of 32,800 ft.

Extreme care was taken with the design and construction of this pressure cabin which had an airtight entrance door and a double-glazed canopy. The seventh and eighth production Ki.102b airframes were fitted with the pressure cabin to serve as prototypes for the Ki.108, the first of these being completed in July 1944 and the second in August. Prior to the commencement of flight trials there was some discussion of the possible effects of a bullet penetrating the pressure cabin. The answer was provided somewhat unexpectedly when, on an early flight test, the entrance door of the pressure cabin suddenly blew out at an altitude of 32,800 feet owing to an insecure lock. The pressure in the cabin dropped suddenly, but the test pilot had the presence

An artist's impression of one of the two Ki.108 high-altitude interceptor prototypes. These were conversions of the seventh and eighth production Ki.102b airframes.

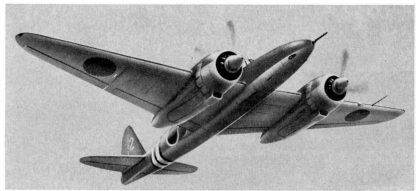

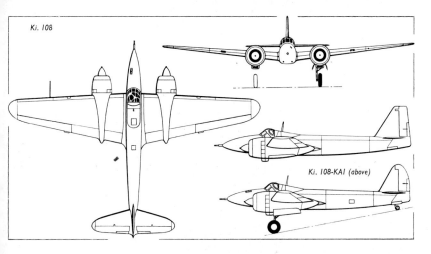

Ki. 108

Ki. 108-KAI (above)

of mind to put the Ki.108 into a dive, landing safely. This accident indicated that the possibility of battle damage at extreme altitudes was not as great a hazard as had been first supposed.

Although trials with the two Ki.108 prototypes were plagued with unexpected troubles developed by the turbo-superchargers of the Mitsubishi Ha.112-IIru fourteen-cylinder radials, the aircraft itself was considered to be a success, and work commenced on the Ki.108-KAI which was a further modification based on the Ki.102c. The Ki.108-KAI featured a similar wing of greater span and area, a lengthened fuselage and redesigned tail surfaces, and two prototypes were built, the first being completed in March 1945 and the second

in May, both being tested by the J.A.A.F.

No production plans had been finalised for either version when Japan capitulated, and the following specification relates to the Ki.108.

Type: *Single-seat High-altitude Interceptor.* **Power Plants:** *Two* 1,500 *h.p. Mitsubishi Ha.112 -IIru fourteen-cylinder radial air-cooled engines.* **Armament:** *One* 37-mm. Ho-203 cannon and two 20-mm. Ho-5 cannon. **Performance:** *Maximum speed,* 360 *m.p.h. at* 32,810 *ft.; time to* 19,685 *ft.,* 18 *min.; service ceiling,* 44,290 *ft.; range,* 1,118 *mls.* **Weights:** *Empty,* 11,684 *lb.; loaded,* 15,873 *lb.* **Dimensions:** *Span,* 51 *ft.* 5 *in.; length,* 38 *ft.* 5 *in.; height,* 12 *ft.* 1⅝ *in.; wing area,* 365.973 *sq. ft.*

37

KYUSHU J7W1 SHINDEN   JAPAN

Conceived as a short-range interceptor at the Yokosuka Air Technical Depot and built by the Kyushu Hikoki K.K., the J7W1 Shinden (Magnificent Lightning) was one of the very few fighters of "canard" configuration to be developed during World War II, the others being the S.A.I. S.S.4 (see page 186, Volume II) and the Curtiss XP-55 Ascender (see Volume IV). The feasibility of the canard arrangement had been proven by three tail-first gliders designated MXY6 and built by the Chigasaki Manufacturing Company. Tests with these were conducted late in 1943 at the J.N.A.F. Aeronautical Engineering Arsenal.

Under the designation X-18, the fighter's design was initiated at the Yokosuka Depot early in 1943, and allocated the designation J7W1 and the name Shinden, the fighter was accepted by the J.N.A.F. and ordered "off the drawing board", and plans were laid for mass production even before the completion of the prototype. Construction of two prototypes of the Shinden commenced at Kyushu's Zasshonokuma factory on June 4, 1944, stress

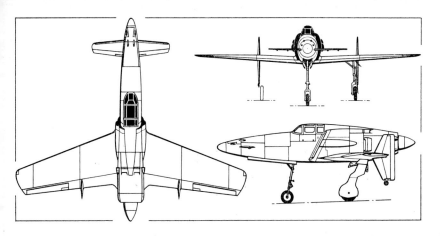

calculations were completed in January 1945, and the first prototype was test flown on August 3, 1945 at the Mushiroda J.A.A.F. base in Northern Kyushu. By this time, both Kyushu's Zasshonokuma factory and Nakajima's Handa factory had reached advanced tooling stages for the J7W1 Shinden, and it was anticipated that the Kyushu and Nakajima plants would respectively attain a monthly production rate of 30 and 120 fighters during 1946, manufacturing 1,086 Shinden fighters between April 1946 and March 1947.

Initial flight tests were relatively successful, although faults included a marked torque pull to starboard and some flutter of the six-blade pusher airscrew. Tabs fitted to the ailerons were expected to rectify the first fault, and modifications to the engine cowling and rear

fuselage were expected to eliminate the blade flutter. The second prototype was never flown, being barely completed when Japan capitulated.

Type: *Single-seat Short-range Interceptor Fighter.* **Power Plant:** *One 2,130 h.p. Mitsubishi Ha.43-42 eighteen-cylinder radial air-cooled engine.* **Armament:** *Four 30-mm. Type 5 cannon, with 60 r.p.g. plus four 66-lb. or 132-lb. bombs.* **Performance:** *Maximum speed, 466 m.p.h. at 28,540 ft.; economical cruising speed, 263 m.p.h. at 13,100 ft.; normal range, 528 mls.; time to 26,250 ft., 10 min. 40 sec.; service ceiling, 39,000 ft.* **Weights:** *Empty, 7,639 lb.; normal loaded, 10,913 lb.; maximum, 11,526 lb.* **Dimensions:** *Span, 36 ft. 5½ in.; length, 30 ft. 4½ in.; height, 12 ft. 10⅝ in.; wing area, 220.66 sq. ft.*

MITSUBISHI A5M4 (CLAUDE) JAPAN

Evolved to a 9-*Shi* (1934) requirement, the Mitsubishi Type 96 Carrier Fighter, or A5M, was the first fighter monoplane to be accepted by the J.N.A.F. and was still standard carrier equipment when the Pacific War began, not being fully replaced as a first-line aircraft until the summer of 1942. The J.N.A.F. 9-*Shi*

specification called for a maximum speed in excess of 218 m.p.h. at 10,000 ft., the ability to attain an altitude of 16,400 ft. in less than 6.5 minutes, and an armament of two 7.7-mm. machine guns. The Nakajima Kotobuki (Congratulation) 5 radial air-cooled engine rated at 550 h.p. was selected for installation in the first prototype which was flown for the first time on February 4, 1935, only eleven months after the inception of the design.

During trials, the new fighter, which bore the manufacturer's designation Ka-14, attained 279 m.p.h. at 10,500 ft., and climbed to 16,400 ft. in 5 min. 54 sec. After the completion of the initial flight test phase, it was decided that, owing to pitching oscillation and a tendency to balloon when landing, the first prototype would be used for structural tests, and the

(Above and below) The A5M2a Model 24. This was a standard J.N.A.F. fighter in the late '30s.

A5M4 Model 34 with the Kotobuki 3-KAI.

flight programme continued with the second prototype. This differed from its predecessor in having a straight wing in place of the original inverted gull wing and a 560 h.p. direct-drive Kotobuki 3, the reduction gears of the Kotobuki 5 being considered inadequately developed for service use. This prototype was also fitted with split flaps, and a similar prototype was evaluated by the J.A.A.F. as the Ki.18 in the autumn and winter of 1935. Further prototypes were built with the Nakajima Hikari (Splendour) 1 engine rated at 700 h.p., but when, in 1936, the J.N.A.F. accepted the aircraft for service as the A5M1 Type 96 Carrier Fighter, Model 1, the 585 h.p. Kotobuki 2-KAI-1 was chosen, armament comprising two 7.7-mm. Type 89 machine guns.

In 1937, the A5M2a Model 21 with the 610 h.p. Kotobuki 2-KAI-3 was placed in production, this becoming the most important J.N.A.F. fighter in the Sino-Japanese conflict. The A5M2b Model 22 had the Kotobuki 3 engine of similar power and an enclosed cockpit, but when this variant entered service in the late summer of 1937, pilots complained that performance was inferior to that of the earlier version, and they distrusted the enclosed cockpit. The A5M2b was, therefore,

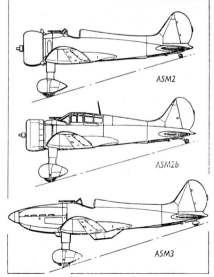

A5M2

A5M2b

A5M3

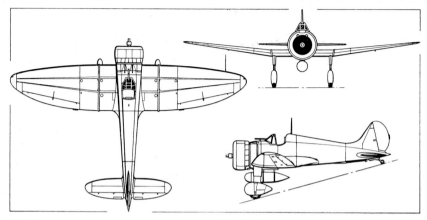

withdrawn from service, and the enclosed cockpit was discarded on subsequent production models. The A5M3 Model 23 was an experimental model with a 610 h.p. Hispano-Suiza 12Xcrs engine and a 20-mm. cannon firing through the airscrew hub, and the next production model was the A5M4 Model 24.

The A5M4 which entered production in 1938 had a 710 h.p. Kotobuki 41 engine driving a three-blade airscrew, and this model was the standard J.N.A.F. fighter when the Pacific War began. The A5M4 Model 34 had a Kotobuki 3-KAI engine, and the A5M4-K

Model 44 was a two-seat training variant. Nearly 800 Type 96 fighters were manufactured by Mitsubishi, and a further 200 were produced by the Watanabe Tekkosho K.K. and the 21st Naval Air Arsenal near Sasebo. By the summer of 1942, the A5M4 had been entirely relegated to second-line and training units.

Type: *Single-seat Shipboard Fighter.* **Power Plant:** *One* 710 *h.p. Nakajima Kotobuki* 41 *nine-cylinder radial air-cooled engine.* **Armament:** *Two* 7.7-mm. *Type* 89 *machine guns plus two* 66-lb. *bombs.* **Performance:** *Maximum speed,* 273 *m.p.h. at* 9,840 *ft.; maximum range (with one* 35 *Imp. gal. auxiliary tank),* 746 *mls. at* 248 *m.p.h.; time to* 9,840 *ft.,* 3 *min.* 35 *sec.; service ceiling,* 32,150 *ft.* **Weights:** *Empty,* 2,681 *lb.; normal loaded,* 3,684 *lb.; max.,* 3,763 *lb.* **Dimensions:** *Span,* 36 *ft.* 1 *in.; length,* 24 *ft.* 9½ *in.; height,* 10 *ft.* 6 *in.; wing area,* 191.597 *sq. ft.*

MITSUBISHI A6M1-3 ZERO-SEN (ZEKE)   JAPAN

The Zero-Sen (Type O Fighter) marked the beginning of a new epoch in naval aviation: it was the first shipboard fighter capable of besting its land-based opponents. More Zero-Sens were produced than any other Japanese warplane, and although its value as a fighter steadily declined as improved Allied types appeared, it emerged as the most famous Japanese aircraft of the Second World War.

Designed by Jiro Horikoshi to a 12-*Shi* requirement for an A5M replacement, the first prototype Zero-Sen flew on April 1, 1939 with a 780 h.p. Mitsubishi MK2 Zuisei (Auspicious Star) 13 fourteen-cylinder radial and, on April 26th, attained a speed of 304 m.p.h. at a gross weight of 5,140 lb. This prototype was accepted by the J.N.A.F. on September 14, 1939 as the A6M1, and a similarly-powered second prototype was flown in October 1939.

In the meantime, the navy had decided to adopt the Nakajima NK1C Sakae (Prosperity) 12 engine rated at 925 h.p. This power plant was only slightly larger and heavier than the Zuisei, and was installed in the third Zero-Sen prototype which flew for the first time on January 18, 1940 under the designation A6M2. With the increased power, the Zero-Sen more than fulfilled the original performance requirements.

The A6M2 Zero-Sen Model 21, seven hundred and forty of which were built by Mitsubishi.

A captured A6M3 Type 0 Model 32 with the Sakae 21 and clipped wingtips.

Before the completion of trials with the third and fourth prototypes, the J.N.A.F. broke with established procedure and requested the delivery of fifteen pre-production A6M2 for operational use in China. Two fighter squadrons were organised and, with the fifteen A6M2s, left Japan for Hankow on July 21, 1940. Ten days later, the A6M2 was officially adopted by the J.N.A.F. as the Type O Carrier Fighter, Model 11. The A6M2 fighters first appeared over Chungking in August 1940, destroying all the defending fighters, and were subsequently used extensively over China despite their limited numbers. General Chennault, impressed by the Zero-Sen's capabilities, attempted to warn the U.S.A.A.F. of the new fighter, but the fact that his warning was totally ignored was demonstrated by the complete surprise evinced by the U.S. forces when this fighter was first encountered in the Pacific.

Production of the Zero-Sen had been initiated by Mitsubishi's Nagoya plant, and delivery tempo rose rapidly. Sixty-four Type O Model 11 fighters were delivered, commencing in December 1939, and these were followed by the A6M2 Model 21, the wings of which

were modified to permit twenty inches of each tip to fold upwards to facilitate carrier stowage. Seven hundred and forty Model 21 Zero-Sen fighters were produced by Mitsubishi, and the Koizuma plant of Nakajima joined the production programme for this variant in November 1941. More than four hundred Zero-Sen fighters had been delivered to the J.N.A.F. when the Pacific War began on December 7, 1941.

Five months before Japan launched the Pacific War, a new version of the Zero-Sen began flight trials. Flown for the first time in June 1941 and designated A6M3, the new model was powered by a 1,130 h.p. Sakae 21 with a two-speed supercharger. To simplify production, the folding wingtips were removed, reducing overall span by 3.28 ft., together with the aileron tabs after the delivery of the first few Sakae 21-powered machines, and in this form the A6M3 entered service as the Type O Fighter Model 32. The results of the reduction in wing span were a marginal decrease in climb rate, a slight increase in turning radius, a 1.8 m.p.h. increase in maximum speed, better roll characteristics and improved aileron effec-

44

tiveness. Early in 1942, the A6M3 was modified by the installation of fuel tanks in the wings as the Model 22, and the full span and folding wingtips were reinstated. Mitsubishi built 560 Model 22 and 343 Model 32 Zero-Sen fighters. These figures were exclusive of the Nakajima production.

Early in 1942 a two-seat conversion trainer variant of the A6M2 Model 21 was produced as the A6M2-K Zero-Rensen, 236 subsequently being built by the 21st Naval Air Arsenal at Sasebo and a further 272 by Hitachi's Chiba plant. Nakajima also evolved a float fighter variant as the A6M2-N, 327 examples of which were built at Nakajima's Koizuma factory.

The successive appearance of the Zero-Sen over every major battle area during the opening stages of the war gave the erroneous impression that the J.N.A.F. possessed unlimited supplies of this remarkable fighter, but by 1943 the A6M2 and A6M3 versions of the Zero-Sen were becoming outclassed by more modern Allied fighters.

The following specification relates to the A6M2 Model 21, figures in parentheses referring to the A6M3 Model 32.

The A6M3 Type 0 Model 22 in which the full wingspan and folding tips were reinstated.

This A6M2 Type 0 Model 21 was the first Zero-Sen to be acquired by the U.S.A. From the carrier Ryujo, *it landed on the island of Aktan.*

Type: *Single-seat Shipboard Interceptor Fighter*

and Fighter-bomber. **Power Plant:** *One 925 (1,130) h.p. Nakajima Sakae 12 (21) fourteen-cylinder radial air-cooled engine.* **Armament:** *Two 7.7-mm. Type 97 machine guns with 500 r.p.g., and two 20-mm. Type 99 cannon with 60 r.p.g. plus two 66-lb. or 132-lb. bombs.* **Performance:** *Maximum speed, 332 (334) m.p.h. at 16,570 ft., 336 (338) m.p.h. at 19,685 ft.; cruising speed, 207 m.p.h. at 13,120 ft.; time to 19,685 ft., 7 min. 27 sec. (7 min. 19 sec.); initial climb rate, 4,517 (4,500) ft./min.; service ceiling, 33,790 (36,250) ft.* **Weights:** *Empty, 3,704 (3,984) lb.; loaded, 5,313 (5,609) lb.* **Dimensions:** *Span, 39 ft. 4½ in.; (36 ft. 1 in.) length, 29 ft. 8¾ in.; height, 11 ft. 5¾ in.; wing area, 241.542 (231.746) sq. ft.*

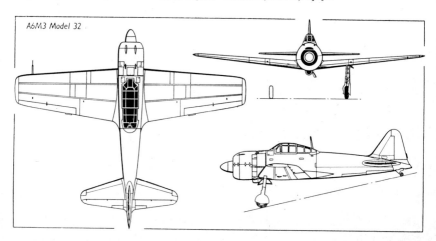

A6M3 Model 32

MITSUBISHI A6M5-8 ZERO-SEN (ZEKE)　　　　JAPAN

With the Battle of Midway the tide of war had turned against Japan. The J.N.A.F. was losing the aerial supremacy gained by the Zero-Sen from the opening days of the Pacific War, and by 1943 the shortcomings of the Mitsubishi fighter were manifest. The J.N.A.F.'s new series of fighters had yet to materialise, and since there was little prospect of more modern fighters becoming available in quantity for many months, attempts had to be made to improve the capabilities of the Zero-Sen. The first of the new models was the A6M5 Model 52, essentially a compromise between performance and produceability.

The A6M5, the prototype of which was completed in August 1943, was based to a large extent upon the earlier A6M3 Model 32.

The wing of reduced span was retained but the wingtips were rounded, and the Sakae 21 was fitted with individual exhaust stacks to provide some thrust augmentation. Despite an increase of 416 lb. in loaded weight, the A6M5 attained a maximum speed of 351 m.p.h. at 19,685 ft. The A6M5 entered production as the Type O Fighter, Model 52, and more Zero-Sens of this variant were produced than any other model, production being undertaken both by Mitsubishi and Nakajima. Mitsubishi alone completed 747 of the original A6M5 model, and plans were prepared to produce the type at Hitachi, but Japan capitulated before any production aircraft had been delivered by this company.

The A6M5 very rapidly became the most

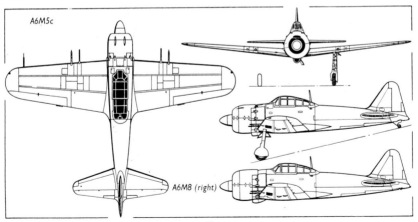

A6M5c

A6M8 (right)

47

Derived from the A6M3 Model 32, the A6M5 (above) entered production as the Type 0 Model 52.

numerous of Japanese fighters, and as the war progressed combat experience and delays in the development of later types dictated changes. The J.N.A.F. consistently demanded a complete revision of the basic Zero-Sen design to raise it to Allied standards, but Mitsubishi's design staff were preoccupied with the development of the 17-*Shi* Reppu, and so the demand went unheeded, the J.N.A.F. being forced to make do with adaptations of the basic aircraft. The first revised model was the A6M5a Model 52a in which the wing was modified to take Mk.4 cannon with belt-feed in place of the earlier magazine-fed Mk.3s, the gain being twenty-five shells per cannon. The first production deliveries of this modified version began in March 1944, and 391 machines were produced by the parent company.

The A6M5b developed in parallel with the A6M5a enjoyed an increase in both firepower and pilot protection. One of the 7.7-mm.

machine guns in the fuselage decking was replaced by a 12.7-mm. gun, armour glass was added to the cockpit canopy, and automatic fire extinguishers were installed. The A6M5b went into production in April 1944, the J.N.A.F. hoping to have the improved fighter available in time to participate in "Operation AGO" (the Battle of the Philippines which began on June 19, 1944), and 470 fighters of this type were produced by Mitsubishi.

Mitsubishi proposed the installation of the more powerful Kinsei 62 engine for the A6M5c Model 52c which had additional armament, armour, fuel tankage and bomb racks, but the Navy refused to accept this proposal and, instead, suggested the installation of an improved Sakae with water-methanol injection. The improved engine was too late to be installed in production A6M5c Zero-Sen fighters which, in consequence, retained the Sakae 21. It was thus radically underpowered and production was terminated after the completion of ninety-three aircraft. The armament pattern of two 13-mm. and two 20-mm. guns in the wings plus a 13-mm. gun in the fuselage introduced by the A6M5c was, however, adhered to by all subsequent versions of the Zero-Sen produced in quantity.

When the long-awaited water-methanol-boosted Sakae 31 eventually became available late in 1944, the more powerful engine was installed in A6M6c Model 53c. This was similar to the unsuccessful A6M5c apart from the engine and the addition of self-sealing wing tanks. It also featured two launching rails for air-to-air rocket missiles under each wing. Apart from one prototype, all A6M6c Zero-Sens were manufactured at Nakajima's Koizuma plant. The A6M7 Model 63, production of which commenced in May 1945, was a fighter/dive-bomber carrying a 550-lb. bomb under the fuselage and two underwing drop-tanks. The tailplane of this model was strengthened, and production was undertaken by both Mitsubishi and Nakajima.

The final production model of the Zero-Sen was a radical departure from its predecessors insofar as the engine was concerned, this being changed for the first time since the fighter had entered production. Owing to shortages of Sakae power plants as a result of U.S. bombing

The A6M6c (below) was fitted with the Sakae 31 and was built by Nakajima at Koizuma.

The A6M5 Type 0 Model 52 was built in larger numbers than any other variant of the Zero-Sen.

attacks on the factories producing these engines, the J.N.A.F. finally agreed to the installation of the Mitsubishi MK8K Kinsei 62 of 1,500 h.p. Work therefore began in November 1944 on the A6M8c Model 64c with the new engine. The forward fuselage was completely redesigned and strengthened to absorb the increased power and larger diameter of the Kinsei. Additional fuel tankage and automatic fire extinguishers were added, and the fuselage armament was removed, leaving a wing-mounted armament of two 13.2-mm. Type 3 machine guns and two 20-mm. Type 99 Mark 4 cannon. The first prototype A6M8c was flown in April 1945, and accepted by the J.N.A.F. during the following month. Construction was consigned to Mitsubishi's dispersed Suzuka, Shimonosho, and Omi plants, as well as Nakajima's Wakaguri, Shizuna and Koizuma plants, and it was proposed to produce 6,300 A6M8c Zero-Sen fighters during 1946, but the war ended before

any production machine was completed.

Mitsubishi produced 3,879 Zero-Sen fighters and Nakajima built a further 6,215 machines.

The following specification relates to the A6M6c Model 53c, data in parentheses referring to the A6M8c Model 64c.

Type: *Single-seat Interceptor Fighter and Fighter-bomber.* **Power Plant:** *One 1,130 (1,560) h.p. Nakajima Sakae 31 (Mitsubishi Kinsei 62) fourteen-cylinder radial air-cooled engine.* **Armament:** *Two 20-mm. Type 99 Mark 4 cannon and three (two) 13.2-mm. Type 3 machine guns.* **Performance:** *Maximum speed, 346 (356) m.p.h. at 19,680 ft., 289 m.p.h. at sea level; cruising speed (75% power), 201 (248) m.p.h.; initial climb rate, 3,140 ft./min.; time to 19,685 (26,240) ft., 7.8 (6.5) min.; service ceiling, 35,100 (36,745) ft.* **Weights:** *Empty, 4,175 (4,740) lb.; loaded, 6,047 (6,944) lb.* **Dimensions:** *Span, 36 ft. 1 in.; length, 29 ft. 9 in.; height, 9 ft. 2 in.; wing area, 229.271 sq. ft.*

MITSUBISHI A7M1-2 REPPU (SAM)   JAPAN

The M-50 Reppu (Hurricane) was designed by Jiro Horikoshi to meet the requirements of the 17-*Shi* shipboard fighter specification which demanded a maximum speed of not less than 397 m.p.h. at 19,685 ft., and the ability to climb to that altitude within approximately six minutes. The 17-*Shi* requirement was issued to Mitsubishi on July 6, 1942, but initial design studies had, in fact, commenced in 1940 with the issue of the 16-*Shi* shipboard fighter requirement, a shortage of design personnel and preoccupation with modifications to production types having seriously delayed the development programme. Jiro Horikoshi felt most strongly that the desired performance could be attained only by use of the Mitsubishi MK9A or MK9B engine, but in September 1942 the Navy officially informed Mitsubishi that the lower-powered Nakajima NK9K Homare (Honour) engine was to be installed in the M-50 Reppu which received the designation A7M1.

Serious delays in prototype construction arose from the priority allocated to A6M Zero-Sen and J2M Raiden modifications and, thus, the first A7M1 prototype did not fly until May 6, 1944. Trials revealed that the fighter possessed excellent stability and controllability but was decidedly underpowered. The NK9K Homare 22 engine was rated at 1,990 h.p. for take-off, but power fell off rapidly with altitude until, at 19,685 ft., the engine was only yielding some 1,300 h.p. Ten minutes were required by the A7M1 to attain this

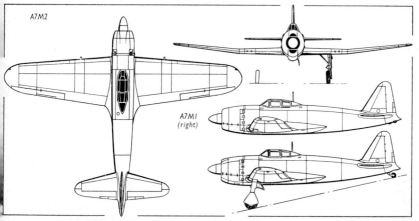

A7M2

A7M1
(right)

51

An impression of the A7M2 Reppu Type A Fighter.

altitude at which maximum speed was only 345 m.p.h.

On July 30, 1944, it was decided to discontinue the further development of the Homare-powered Reppu, and shortly afterwards the Navy reluctantly gave permission for the installation of the Mitsubishi MK9A in the sixth prototype Reppu airframe which, thus, became the first prototype A7M2. The first test flight with the new engine was made on October 13, 1944, and it was immediately obvious that manoeuvrability, climb rate, and maximum speed were notably improved while stability and controllability were unimpaired. Production was immediately authorised as the A7M2 Reppu Type A Fighter, Model 22, and it was anticipated that the first production machines would be delivered in April 1945. However, in December 1944 the Nagoya district in which production of the Reppu was centred was shattered by an earthquake, and this, following several damaging air attacks, completely disrupted the production programme. Air attacks on the Daiko engine plant, which was responsible for the Mitsubishi MK9A power plant production, reduced deliveries to a trickle. Six additional prototypes of the A7M2 were completed and flown, and the first production Reppu was completed, but further air attacks brought the whole programme to a halt.

At the time of Japan's capitulation, prototypes of two developments of the Reppu had been nearing completion. These were the A7M3-J Reppu-Kai high-altitude interceptor, the prototype of which was scheduled to be completed in October 1945, and the A7M3 Reppu Model 23 scheduled to commence tests in August 1945. The A7M3-J was to have had an MK9A engine with an exhaust-driven turbo-supercharger and giving 2,130 h.p. at 22,310 ft. and 1,920 h.p. at 33,800 ft. The turbo-supercharger installation demanded a number of changes to the fuselage, and the inboard wing sections were redesigned in order to accommodate an armament of four 30-mm. cannon. Estimated performance included a maximum speed of 403 m.p.h. at 33,800 ft.

The A7M3, development of which proceeded in parallel, differed from the A7M2 principally in having an MK9C engine with a mechanically driven three-speed supercharger. The wing-folding mechanism was eliminated and wing-mounted armament was increased to six 20-mm. cannon. The following specification relates to the A7M2.

Type: *Single-seat Shipboard Interceptor Fighter and Fighter-bomber.* **Power Plant:** *One 2,200 h.p. Mitsubishi MK9A eighteen-cylinder radial air-cooled engine.* **Armament:** *Four 20-mm. Type 99-II cannon with 200 r.p.g. or two 20-mm. Type 99-II cannon with 200 r.p.g. and two 13.2-mm. Type 3 machine guns with 400 r.p.g., plus two 132-lb. bombs.* **Performance:** *Maximum speed, 390 m.p.h. at 21,650 ft.; range (with two 77 Imp. gal. drop tanks), 976 mls. at 259 m.p.h. at 9,840 ft., (on internal fuel) 570 mls.; normal endurance, 2.2 hr.; climb to 19,685 ft., 6 min. 7 sec., to 32,810 ft., 15 min. 20 sec.; ceiling, 35,760 ft.* **Weights:** *Empty, 6,834 lb.; loaded, 10,405 lb.* **Dimensions:** *Span, 45 ft. 11 in.; length, 36 ft. 0½ in.; height, 14 ft. 0½ in.; wing area, 332.174 sq. ft.*

MITSUBISHI J2M2-7 RAIDEN (JACK)   JAPAN

The Raiden (Thunderbolt) denoted a radical change in Japanese single-seat fighter concepts. For the first time, manoeuvrability became a secondary consideration to speed and climb rate whereas, previously, it had been considered of paramount importance. Again, the Raiden was the first Japanese fighter to be designed from the outset purely for the interception role. Under the designation M-20, design of the Raiden began under the direction of Jiro Horikoshi in 1940 as part of the 14-*Shi* programme. The Mitsubishi Kasei (Mars) radial was chosen to power the new fighter and, to reduce drag, was fitted with an extension shaft to permit a finely tapered cowling, an engine-driven fan drawing the air through a narrow annular intake. A liminar-flow aerofoil section was selected for the wing, and so-called "combat" flaps were fitted to increase lift with the minimum of drag. An extremely shallow, curved windscreen was adopted for the cockpit, and forged components were used extensively in the structure.

Designated J2M1, the first prototype Raiden was powered by a 1,460 h.p. MK4C Kasei 13 engine driving a three-blade variable-pitch VDM airscrew, and was flown for the first time on March 20, 1942. Stability and controllability were praised by the manufacturer's test pilots, but it was complained that forward view was totally inadequate, that the curved windscreen distorted view for landing, and that the main undercarriage members would not retract at speeds above 100 m.p.h. Throughout June and July the J2M1 was tested by the Navy at the Suzuka Naval Air Base, and the principal criticisms concerned the inadequate field of vision, the unsatisfactory operation of the airscrew pitch-change mechanism, and the fact that both speed and climb rate (357 m.p.h.

One of the three J2M1 prototypes the first of which was flown on March 20, 1942, with a Kasei 13.

(*Above and left*) *The J2M3 Raiden 21 with four wing-mounted 20-mm. cannon.*

at 19,685 ft. and 7.8 min. to that altitude) were below those specified.

As the specified performance could not be attained with the MK4C Kasei 13, the fourth airframe was adapted to take the MK4R-A Kasei 23a which, with methanol-water injection, provided 1,820 h.p. for take-off. With the more powerful engine the Raiden became the J2M2, and other changes included the provision of a four-blade airscrew, the introduction of new exhaust stacks which provided a certain amount of jet thrust, and a taller cockpit canopy embodying optically flat panels. In October 1942 the Navy adopted the modified fighter as the J2M2 Raiden Interceptor, Model 11, but the test programme ran anything but smoothly. Considerable effort was expended in eliminating vibration in the airscrew extension shaft, and at maximum power the Kasei 23a ran roughly, vibrated seriously and emitted a considerable amount of smoke. Engine vibration was somewhat reduced by modification of the engine mount shock absorbers, while the excessive smoke was eliminated by adjustments to the fuel and methanol-water injection systems. Vibration remained a problem, however, until it was eventually discovered that it could be suppressed by increasing the resilience of the engine-mount shock absorbers and the rigidity of the airscrew blades.

The second production J2M2 Raiden crashed on June 16, 1943 in temporarily inexplicable circumstances shortly after becoming airborne. The fighter had nosed down suddenly from some seventy feet, and a similar phenomenon was experienced with the tenth J2M2. Fortunately, the pilot of the latter aircraft immediately extended the undercarriage and, upon landing, it was ascertained that the tailwheel shock strut had pressed against the elevator torque-tube lever as it retracted, jamming the control column forward! In January 1944 the thirtieth J2M2 disintegrated over Toyohashi airfield and, although the cause of this accident was not satisfactorily explained, it was believed that violent vibration in the engine resulting from a broken attachment point had resulted in a secondary airframe failure. Another possibility was that the engine cowling had detached itself and hit the tail assembly. The engine attachment points were reinforced and the cowling fasteners strengthened, but other Raidens disintegrated in mid-air *after* these modifications had been made.

The 381st Air Corps at Toyohashi had received the first J2M2 Raiden fighters in December 1943 for pilot familiarisation, and by this time the J2M2 had been supplanted by the J2M3 Raiden 21, 155 examples of the initial production model having been delivered. The J2M3 differed from its predecessor principally in armament. Whereas the initial production model had carried two fuselage-mounted 7.7-mm. machine guns and two

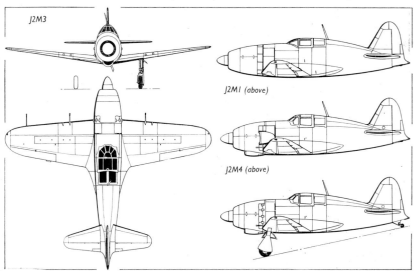

J2M3

J2M1 (above)

J2M4 (above)

*(Above and on opposite page) The J2M3a Raiden 21a with four wing-mounted
Type 99-IIs.*

wing-mounted 20-mm. Type 99-I cannon, the
J2M3 had the 7.7-mm. guns eliminated and the
wing cannon supplemented by a pair of faster-
firing 20-mm. Type 99-II cannon. With the
adoption of four Type 99-II cannon as standard,
the designation was changed to J2M3a Raiden
21a. A new domed cockpit canopy was introduced on the production line in June 1944 in
answer to pilots' continued complaints over
poor vision in combat. With the new canopy
the J2M3 and J2M3a became respectively the
J2M6 and J2M6a Raiden 31 and 31a.

In an attempt to improve the Raiden's capabilities as a high-altitude interceptor, two
prototypes were built with turbo-superchargers
under the designation J2M4 Raiden 32, the
first of these flying in August 1944. The four

wing-mounted 20-mm. cannon were supplemented with two 20-mm. cannon in the upper
decking of the forward fuselage, and maximum
speed was 363 m.p.h. at 30,185 ft., but the
somewhat complex turbo-supercharger had
faults which could not be quickly eliminated,
and the J2M4 was abandoned in favour of the
J2M5 Raiden 33. First flown in May 1944,
the J2M5 had the MK4U-A Kasei 26a engine
with a mechanically-driven supercharger and a
larger intake manifold. The J2M5 carried only
two 20-mm. cannon which were mounted in
the wings, but performance included maximum
speeds of 381 m.p.h. at 21,600 ft. and 375
m.p.h. at 26,250 ft., and altitudes of 19,685 ft.
and 26,250 ft. were attained in 6 min. 20 sec.
and 9 min. 45 sec. respectively. The J2M5 was

immediately placed in production at Mitsubishi's Suzuka plant and at the Koza Naval Air Arsenal, but despite the most strenuous efforts, only between thirty and forty fighters of this type were completed owing to the limited supplies of Kasei 26a engines, but these were immediately assigned to operational units, proving themselves among the most effective interceptors to be employed against the B-29 Superfortresses. The Kasei 26a was also installed in some Raiden 21 and 21a airframes which were redesignated J2M7 and J2M7a Raiden 23 and 23a.

The original Raiden production programme for 1944 had called for the delivery of 3,600 aircraft and the attainment of a production rate of 500 aircraft per month by the end of that year. In fact, hardly more than 500 Raidens of all types had been completed by the end of the war. Plagued by teething troubles and production difficulties throughout its life, the Raiden was, nevertheless, a sound design basically. The Raiden, which made its operational début during the Battle of the Marianas in September 1944 and fought in the defence of Japan's home islands until the end, enjoyed a steep climbing angle and rapid climb rate. Handling and control was good at all speeds

from the stall to 325 m.p.h., although the ailerons tended to be heavy above this speed. Stability was excellent, and although there was little stall warning the stalling characteristics were exceptional, recovery being very rapid with very little loss of altitude. There was no tendency to spin, and manoeuvrability was good.

The following specification relates to the J2M3 Raiden 21.

Type: Single-seat Interceptor Fighter. **Power Plant:** *One 1,820 h.p. Mitsubishi MK4R-A Kasei 23a fourteen-cylinder radial air-cooled engine.* **Armament:** *Two 20-mm. Type 99-I and two 20-mm. Type 99-II cannon with 100 r.p.g., plus two 66-lb. or 132-lb. bombs.* **Performance:** *Maximum speed, 338 m.p.h. at 7,875 ft., 365 m.p.h. at 17,390 ft., 371 m.p.h. at 19,360 ft.; cruising speed, 219 m.p.h. at 9,840 ft., 265 m.p.h. at 19,685 ft.; range (with 26 Imp. gal. drop tank), 655 mls. at 265 m.p.h. at 19,685 ft.; time to 9,840 ft., 2 min. 56 sec., to 19,685 ft., 5 min. 40 sec.; service ceiling, 38,385 ft.* **Weights:** *Empty, 5,423 lb.; normal loaded, 7,573 lb.; maximum, 8,699 lb.* **Dimensions:** *Span, 35 ft. 5¼ in.; length, 32 ft. 7⅞ in.; height, 12 ft. 8⅝ in.; wing area, 215.816 sq. ft.*

MITSUBISHI KI.83　　　　　　　　　　　　　　　　　　JAPAN

In 1943 the J.A.A.F. awarded the Mitsubishi Jokogyo K.K. a contract for the design and development of a heavily-armed long-range high-altitude fighter. The design team to which the task was allocated, headed by Tomio Kubo who had previously designed the Ki.46 "Shin-Shitei" reconnaissance aircraft, attempted to meet the requirement with a single-engined aircraft, but as no single power plant with a suitable performance was available, a twin-engined layout was adopted at an early stage in the programme.

Powered by two turbo-supercharged Ha.211ru radial engines rated at 2,200 h.p. for take-off and 1,930 h.p. at 16,400 ft., the Ki.83 was an exceptionally clean two-seat all-metal stressed-skin mid-wing monoplane with a heavy forward-firing armament comprising two 30-mm. Ho-105 and two 20-mm. Ho-5 cannon. Two 110-lb. bombs could be carried in a small internal bay. The first of four prototypes was flown in October 1944, and despite the fact that the original specification had not demanded extreme manoeuvrability, the Ki.83 could execute a loop in thirty-one seconds at 403 m.p.h. at 9,500 feet, the diameter of the loop being 2,200 feet. The J.N.A.F. also evinced interest in the Ki.83

Only four prototypes of the Ki.83 interceptor had been completed by the end of the war.

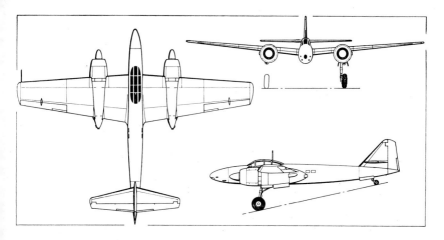

from an early stage in its development, and was to have received a number of aircraft of this type for use as land-based interceptors.

A reconnaissance version of the Ki.83, designated Ki.95, was originally proposed as a replacement for the Ki.46, but this project was abandoned in 1943. The Ki.95 would have been externally similar to the Ki.83, but armament was to be reduced to two 20-mm. Ho-5 cannon, and range and endurance were estimated at 2,175 miles and 7 hr. 30 min. respectively. A further development of the basic Ki.83 design projected during the final months of the war was the Ki.103, but no construction was undertaken.

The four Ki.83 prototypes were still under test at the end of the war, and plans for quantity production had not been finalised.

Type: *Two-seat Long-range High-altitude Interceptor.* **Power Plants:** *Two 2,200 h.p. Mitsubishi Ha.211ru eighteen-cylinder radial air-cooled engines.* **Armament:** *Two 30-mm. Ho-105 cannon and two 20-mm. Ho-5 cannon plus two 110-lb. bombs.* **Performance:** *Maximum speed, 438 m.p.h. at 32,810 ft., 416 m.p.h. at 16,400 ft.; cruising speed, 280 m.p.h. at 13,125 ft.; maximum range, 1,740 mls.; normal range, 1,213 mls.; normal endurance, 4.34 hr.; time to 32,810 ft., 10 min. 30 sec.; service ceiling, 41,535 ft.* **Weights:** *Empty, 13,249 lb.; loaded, 19,687 lb.* **Dimensions:** *Span, 50 ft. 10¼ in.; length, 41 ft. 0 in.; height, 15 ft. 1 in.; wing area, 362.851 sq. ft.*

At an early stage in the development of the Mitsubishi Ki.67 Hiryu bomber the potential merits of the design prompted consideration of the basic design for the long-range escort fighter role. In the summer of 1942 work started on such a variant under the designation Ki.69, and development proceeded in parallel with that of the bomber until J.A.A.F. demands for an increase in the tempo of work on the Ki.67 necessitated the shelving of the Ki.69 project. Work on an escort fighter variant of the Hiryu was resumed more than a year later under the designation Ki.112, only to be abandoned without the construction of a prototype, but in 1944 the possibility of installing a 75-mm. cannon in the nose of a Ki.67 was considered, it being suggested that this combination could make a potent B-29 Superfortress interceptor.

Two standard Ki.67-Ib Hiryu bombers were turned over to the 1st Army Air Arsenal (Tachikawa Dai-ichi Rikugun Kokusho) for modification and testing. The first conversion, known as the Ki.104 experimental interceptor, differed from the Ki.67-Ib solely in having a new nose section in which was mounted the Ho-401 cannon. Initial firing trials indicated

that, providing a suitable mounting could be developed, the aircraft would be capable of firing the large-calibre weapon in the air with an acceptable degree of accuracy. Work began immediately on a second conversion which was intended to serve as a prototype for the production version to be built by Mitsubishi. This had a completely redesigned nose section and cannon mounting, and while testing proceeded, the Ki.109 experimental interceptor designation was assigned to Mitsubishi for the development of a turbo-supercharged version of the Hiryu fighter which would be capable of intercepting the Superfortress at its best operational altitudes.

Work on the Ki.109 started in January 1944, and standard Ki.67-Ib airframes had been modified and were merely awaiting the delivery of their Ha.104ru turbo-supercharged engines when the first Superfortresses arrived over Japan. Owing to Mitsubishi's complete inability to deliver the Ha.104ru engines, it was agreed to fit the initial production batch of Ki.109 interceptors with standard 2,000 h.p. Ha.104 engines, and in August 1944 the first machine was completed, followed by a second in October. A further twenty of these interim

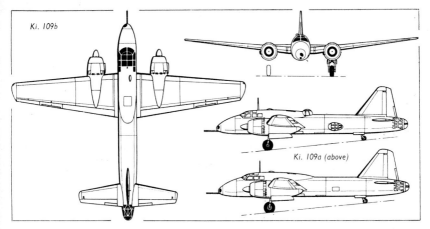

Ki. 109b

Ki. 109a (above)

fighters were delivered in the following few months, and these, designated Ki.109a, retained the original dorsal, waist and tail gun positions of the bomber, although the crew was reduced to four members. Use of the Ho-401 cannon was limited as these aircraft carried only fifteen 75-mm. shells which had to be laboriously loaded by the co-pilot.

Completion of the twenty-second Ki.109a ended reliance on existing Ki.67-Ib airframes, and production continued as the Ki.109b with an extensively modified fuselage built from the ground up as a fighter. The standard Ki.67-Ib wing and tail assemblies and engines were retained, Mitsubishi having still proved incapable of producing the Ha.104ru in quantity, but the fuselage was refined aerodynamically, and the dorsal and waist gun positions were deleted. Armament was confined to the 75-

mm. nose cannon and a single 12.7-mm. gun in the tail. Twenty-two Ki.109b interceptors were built, and these were assigned to combat units. Their combat début proved a dismal failure, however, as without the turbo-superchargers originally specified, they were unable to engage the high-flying B-29s.

Type: *Four-seat Heavy Interceptor.* **Power Plants:** *Two 2,000 h.p. Mitsubishi Ha.104 Type 4 eighteen-cylinder radial air-cooled engines.* **Armament:** *One 75-mm. cannon and one flexible 12.7-mm. Ho-103 machine gun.* **Performance:** *Maximum speed, 342 m.p.h. at 19,980 ft.; range, 1,367 mls.; endurance, 5 hr. 30 min.* **Weights:** *Empty, 16,367 lb.; loaded, 23,810 lb.* **Dimensions:** *Span, 73 ft. 9¾ in.; length, 58 ft. 10¾ in.; height, 15 ft. 9 in.; wing area, 741.094 sq. ft.*

MITSUBISHI J8M1 SHUSUI

Germany's success in adapting the bi-fuel rocket motor as prime mover in a fast-climbing, high-speed target defence interceptor aroused considerable interest in both the J.N.A.F. and J.A.A.F., and, in 1944, for the sum of twenty million Reichsmarks, Japan acquired the manufacturing rights of the Walter HWK 109-509 rocket motor, together with one example of this power plant. The Japanese also acquired a licence for the construction of the Messerschmitt Me 163B (see Volume I, page 171) fighter powered by the HWK 109-509, and the Mitsubishi Jukogyo K.K. was assigned the task of manufacturing the German interceptor. However, these plans received a severe setback when the submarine carrying an example of the Me 163B and full manufacturing details was sunk en route to Japan. The Japanese were thus left with only a simple instructional manual on the interceptor.

Undaunted by this setback, in July 1944 Mitsubishi began the design of an airframe based broadly upon that of the Me 163B

The J8M1 Shusui short-range interceptor was based broadly on the design of the Me 163B. The first prototype flew on July 7, 1945, but crashed shortly after taking-off.

Between fifty and sixty MXY7 Akigusa gliders (above and below) were built by the Maeda company as trainers for the J8M1. These were intended to provide a nucleus of semi-trained pilots, water tanks compensating for the Toku Ro.2 rocket motor and its fuel tanks. Several Akigusa gliders were supplied to the J.A.A.F., which proposed to use the Shusui as the Ki.202.

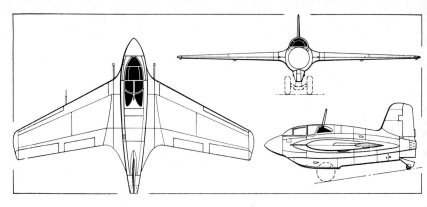

without waiting for further assistance from Germany. In order to provide a nucleus of semi-trained pilots for the rocket-driven interceptor, which had received the J.N.A.F. designation J8M1 and the name Shusui (Rigorous Sword), a number of wooden gliders, similar in size and external appearance to the interceptor and designated MXY7, were built by the Maeda Koku Kenkyusho. Named Akigusa (Autumn Grass), the MXY7 was flown in November 1944, and two of the fifty–sixty gliders of this type built were assigned to Mitsubishi for experimental work on the Shusui, and a few were delivered to the J.A.A.F. which proposed to adopt the Shusui as the Ki.200.

While development of the airframe was proceeding to a 19-*Shi* requirement, both Mitsubishi and the Yokosuka Naval Aeronautical Engineering Arsenal were adapting the HWK 109-509 rocket motor for Japanese production techniques as the Toku Ro.2 (Kr-10), and responsibility for airframe production had been assigned to Mitsubishi, Fuji and Nisson. Early in June 1945 the first Toku Ro.2 rocket motors were delivered to Mitsubishi, and the first J8M1 Shusui was delivered to Yokosuka, flying for the first time on July 7, 1945. The aircraft attained 1,300 feet in a steep climb when the rocket motor failed and the aircraft crashed. The cause of the accident was variously explained as the result of the hydrogen peroxide shifting to the rear of the partially empty tank and cutting the fuel supply, and owing to air entering a fuel pipe and causing a blockage. However, the fuel system was redesigned, but hostilities terminated before the modified sixth and seventh aircraft could be flown. To increase endurance, it was proposed to remove one of the 17-*Shi* 30-mm. cannon and replace this with additional fuel. This variant was to have been known as the J8M2 Shusui-Kai.

Shusui development had been considered as

64

joint J.N.A.F.-J.A.A.F. project from the outset, the J.A.A.F. version of the interceptor being designated Ki.200. This was eventually taken over by the Army Aero-Technical Research Institute (Rikugun Kokugijutsu Kenkyujo) and developed as the Ki.202. This was chosen as the priority J.A.A.F. interceptor project, but no prototype had been completed at the time of Japan's capitulation.

Type: *Single-seat Short-range Interceptor Fighter.* **Power Plant:** *One* 3,300 *lb. Yokosuka Toku Ro.*2 *bi-fuel liquid rocket motor.* **Armament:** *Two* 30-mm. *Type 5 cannon with 60 r.p.g.* **Performance:** *Maximum speed,* 497 *m.p.h. at* 32,810 *ft.; powered endurance,* 5 *min.* 30 *sec.; time to* 19,685 *ft.,* 2 *min.* 10 *sec., to* 32,810 *ft.,* 3 *min.* 30 *sec., to* 39,370 *ft.,* 3 *min.* 50 *sec.* **Weights:** *Empty,* 3,186 *lb.; loaded,* 8,598 *lb.* **Dimensions:** *Span,* 31 *ft.* 2 *in.; length,* 19 *ft.* 2⅜ *in.; height,* 8 *ft.* 10¼ *in.; wing area,* 190.843 *sq. ft.*

Although some five J8M1 prototypes had been completed by the end of the war, only the first machine was actually flown. The J.A.A.F. was to have tested the Shusui as the Ki.200.

The Nakajima Ki.27 single-seat fighter probably did more to raise the Japanese aircraft industry to world standards than any Japanese warplane. In continuous production from mid-1937 until July 1940, and built in larger quantities than any other Japanese combat aircraft of pre-war design, the Ki.27 was the J.A.A.F.'s first low-wing fighter monoplane and the first to employ an enclosed cockpit. Evolved directly from Nakajima's private-venture PE fighter monoplane which, first flown in July 1936, did not find favour with the J.A.A.F., the Ki.27 competed with the Mitsubishi Ki.18 (similar to the A5M1 and the Kawasaki Ki.28 for production orders. The last-mentioned type was the faster, attaining what was, for that time, the phenomenal maximum speed of 303 m.p.h., but the Ki.27 was the most manoeuvrable of the three fighters and as manoeuvrability was considered to be of paramount importance by the J.A.A.F., it was finally selected for production as the standard Army fighter.

Three prototypes of the Ki.27 were built, the first of these, powered by a 650 h.p. Nakajima Ha.1a nine-cylinder radial, flying

Ki.27b Type 97 Model B fighters of the Akeno Fighter Training School.

(Above and right) The Ki.27a, the J.A.A.F.'s first low-wing fighter monoplane in service.

on October 15, 1936. The three prototypes each had wings of different gross areas (176.528 sq. ft., 190.28 sq. ft., and 199.777 sq. ft.), and the largest of these was selected for the ten service test models. To ensure maximum manoeuvrability, an extremely light structure was employed by the Ki.27, and quantity production was initiated in 1937, the type being hurriedly issued to first-line units based in Manchuria during the following year as replacements for the Ki.10 fighter biplane. It was first used in combat during the Nomonhan incident near the north-west border of Manchuria, being employed with considerable success against Russo-Mongolian Polikarpov I-15 fighters. By May 1939, no fewer than five J.A.A.F. wings of Ki.27a Type 97 Fighter, Model A aircraft were in operation against the Russo-Mongolian forces, giving the Japanese a major advan-

tage, but with the assignment of faster Polikarpov I-16 fighter monoplanes, the Ki.27 found itself at a disadvantage in level, climb and dive speeds, although in the traditional "dog-fight" type of combat the Nakajima fighter was the superior machine.

The Ki.27a was supplanted in 1939 by the Ki.27b Type 97 Fighter, Model B. The twin

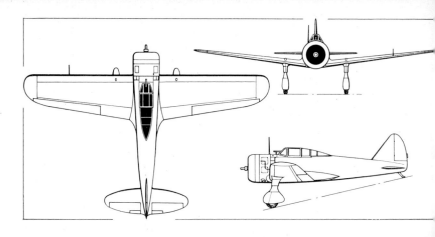

(Above, below, right, and on opposite page) The Ki.27b continued in production until July 1940.

7.7-mm. gun armament was retained, as was also the 650 h.p. Ha.1b engine, but the airframe was generally cleaned up and the cockpit hood was modified. Various internal equipment changes were also made. The Ki.27b was subsequently used extensively in China, and participated in the early fighting over the Philippines, Malaya, Burma and the Dutch East Indies. An improved model, the Ki.27-KAI, was proposed in 1940, and three aircraft were actually built, but by that time preparations were in hand for the production of the Ki.43 Hayabusa, and the last Ki.27 fighters were delivered in July of that year. A total of 3,386 Ki.27 fighters was built, including prototypes, and of these 2,019 were built by the parent company and the remainder by Mansyu Hikoki Seizo K.K. (Manchurian Aircraft Manufacturing Company). In addition to the J.A.A.F., the Manchurian Air Force employed the Ki.27.

Type: *Single-seat Interceptor Fighter and Fighter-bomber.* **Power Plant:** *One 710 h.p. Nakajima Ha.1b nine-cylinder radial air-cooled engine.* **Armament:** *Two 7.7-mm. Type 89 machine guns plus four 55-lb. bombs.* **Performance:** *Maximum speed, 286 m.p.h. at 16,400 ft.; range, 389 mls.; time to 16,400 ft., 5 min. 22 sec.* **Weights:** *Empty, 2,447 lb.; loaded, 3,946 lb.* **Dimensions:** *Span, 37 ft. 1½ in.; length, 24 ft. 8½ in.; height, 9 ft. 2¼ in.; wing area, 199.77 sq. ft.*

NAKAJIMA KI.43 HAYABUSA (OSCAR)   JAPAN

The Hayabusa (Peregrine Falcon) was

numerically the most important Japanese Army Air Force fighter of the war. Despite the fact that, on December 8, 1941, the J.A.A.F. possessed only forty Hayabusa fighters, this warplane appeared in rapid succession over Malaya, Burma, Sumatra and Java during the first six months of the Pacific conflict, and although obsolescent continued in production until Japan's final defeat.

The Nakajima Hikoki K.K. received a development contract in 1938 for a new single-seat fighter to which was allocated the designation Ki.43. Designed by Hideo Ito-kawa, the Ki.43 was powered by the new Nakajima Ha.25 Sakae, and the first of three prototypes was completed in January 1939 at Nakajima's Ota factory. The prototypes carried an armament of two 7.7-mm. Type 89

(Above, left, and below) The Ki.43-Ib entered production in the summer of 1941, supplanting the Ki.43-Ia.

The Ki.43-Ic (above) had twin 12.7-mm. guns and the Ki.43-Ia (below, right) had two 7.7-mm. guns.

machine guns and attained a maximum speed of 323 m.p.h. By comparison with the earlier Nakajima Ki.27, J.A.A.F. pilots found the Ki.43 prototypes to be sluggish on the controls and to possess poor manoeuvrability. Major redesign was therefore undertaken by Nakajima in order to reduce the fighter's weight and improve its characteristics. The wing area was slightly increased and one prototype was fitted with a fixed undercarriage, the weight of the retraction mechanism being considered a dispensable luxury by many at this time. The most important change was the introduction of the so-called "combat" or "battle" flap which, extended in action, provided additional lift, increased the turn rate and improved control response. By means of this innovation, the Ki.43 became one of the most manoeuvrable fighters extant. All controls were extremely sensitive and the fighter was completely devoid of any vicious characteristics. Ten modified machines were built, the first of

these being completed in November 1939, and J.A.A.F. pilots were now highly enthusiastic about the new fighter.

Production of the fighter began at Nakajima's Ota factory, the first model being the Type 1 Fighter Model 1A (Ki.43-Ia) powered by the Ha.25 (later known as the Ha.35/12 under the unified J.A.A.F./J.N.A.F. designation system) rated at 975 h.p. for take-off and possessing a military rating of 955 h.p. at

71

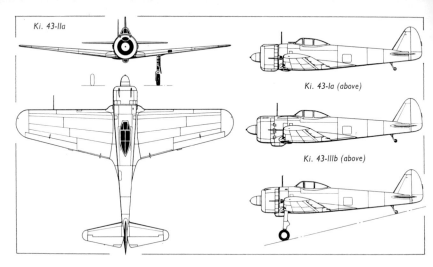

Ki. 43-IIa

Ki. 43-Ia (above)

Ki. 43-IIIb (above)

The Ki.43-IIa (above and on opposite page) began trials in February 1942, five prototypes being built.

11,100 ft. Armament comprised two 7.7-mm. machine guns, and performance included a maximum speed of 304 m.p.h. at 13,120 ft. and a cruising speed of 199 m.p.h. at 8,200 ft. Production of the Ki.43-Ia began in March 1941, and this model was quickly supplanted by the Model 1B (Ki.43-Ib) which carried one 7.7-mm. gun and one 12.7-mm. gun, and the Model 1C (Ki.43-Ic) armed with two 12.7-mm. guns, the last-mentioned version being the first large-scale production model and assigned the popular name of Hayabusa.

Although the Ki.43-I Hayabusa enjoyed considerable success during the early months of the Pacific War, it soon became obvious that more power and increased armour protection were necessary. A rudimentary form of self-sealing fuel tank was introduced, 13-mm. armoured head and back plates were installed in the cockpit, and an improved version of the Ha.25 engine, the Ha.115, was fitted, this being rated at 1,105 h.p. for take-off and possessing a military rating of 1,085 h.p. at 9,200 ft. Five prototypes were built embodying these modifications, the first of these being completed in February 1942, and as the Type 1 Fighter Model 2A (Ki.43-IIa) it entered production at Ota, the earlier model being phased out, the 716th and last Ki.43-I Hayabusa being delivered during the following autumn. The wing span of the Ki.43-IIa was reduced by 4¼ in. from that of the preceding model to 37 ft. 6¼ in., armament comprised two 12.7-mm. guns, and underwing racks were fitted for two 550-lb. bombs.

The Ki.43-IIa was also placed in production by the Tachikawa Hikoki K.K. in May 1943, and prior to this the 1st Army Air Arsenal (Tachikawa Dai-ichi Rikugun Kokusho) began to build the type. In the event, the Arsenal

The Ki.43-IIa (above and below, left) featured some fuel tank and pilot protection, and the Ha.115 engine.

suffered a number of difficulties, and by the time the programme was abandoned in November 1943, only forty-nine Hayabusa fighters had been completed. Further combat experience dictated a number of other changes in the Hayabusa, and between June and August 1942 three prototypes of the Model 2B (Ki.43-IIb) were completed. This model featured clipped wing-tips which reduced overall span to 35 ft. 6¾ in., and entered service in the summer of 1943, serving over every theatre

to which the J.A.A.F. was committed. The Ki.43-IIb was capable of out-manoeuvring every Allied fighter it encountered and its element was dog-fighting, but the P-38 Lightning, the P-47 Thunderbolt and the P-51 Mustang could all out-dive and out-zoom the Japanese fighter which could not withstand the greater firepower of the Allied types, frequently disintegrating in the air when hit.

Despite the obsolescence of the basic design development continued, and in December 1944 production of the Type 1 Fighter Model 3A (Ki.43-IIIa) was begun by both Nakajima and Tachikawa. This model switched to the Mitsubishi Ha.112 (Ha.33/42) Kasei engine rated at 1,250 h.p. and employing individual exhaust stacks to provide a certain amount of exhaust thrust augmentation. Maximum speed was boosted to 342 m.p.h. at 19,188 ft., and the Ki.43-IIIa was assigned to J.A.A.F. interceptor units defending Tokyo and other major

A Ki.43-Ic fighter with crude starter truck at an operational field in 1942.

Japanese cities. The ultimate development was the Model 3B (Ki.43-IIIb) developed by Tachikawa. This was the first model of the Hayabusa to mount large-calibre armament, two 20-mm. cannon supplanting the twin 12.7-mm. guns. The exhaust system was extensively modified and numerous changes were made to the fuselage and wings, but only two prototypes had been completed when the end of the war terminated further development.

When Hayabusa production finished 5,878 machines had been delivered, forty-nine of these having been built by the 1st Arsenal and 2,629 by Tachikawa. The following specification relates to the Type 1 Model 2B (Ki.43-IIb).

Type: *Single-seat Interceptor Fighter and Fighter-bomber.* **Power Plant:** *One* 1,130 *h.p. Nakajima Ha.*115 *(Ha.*35/21*) fourteen-cylinder two-row air-cooled radial engine.* **Armament:** *Two* 12.7-mm. *Type* 1 *machine guns with* 250 *r.p.g., and two* 550-lb. *bombs.* **Performance:** *Maximum speed,* 320 *m.p.h. at* 19,680 *ft.; cruising speed,* 214 *m.p.h. at* 13,125 *ft.; climb to* 16,400 *ft.,* 5 *min.* 49 *sec.; service ceiling,* 36,800 *ft.; normal range,* 1,006 *mls.; ferry range (with maximum external fuel),* 1,865 *mls.; maximum endurance,* 7.6 *hr.* **Weights :** *Empty,* 3,812 *lb.; normal loaded,* 5,320 *lb.; max.,* 5,874 *lb.* **Dimensions:** *Span,* 35 *ft.* 6¾ *in.; length,* 29 *ft.* 3 *in.; height,* 10 *ft.* 1½ *in.; wing area,* 232 *sq. ft.*

NAKAJIMA KI.44 SHOKI (TOJO)   JAPAN

Design of the Ki.44 Shoki (Demon) fighter was commenced shortly after that of the Ki.43 Hayabusa, but whereas the Hayabusa placed emphasis on manoeuvrability, this feature was considered to be of secondary importance in the design of the Shoki which stressed speed and climb rate, thus denoting a radical change in Japanese fighter design thinking. Considered as a heavy interceptor, the Shoki was flown for the first time in August 1940, and ten prototypes were built. After a series of comparative trials between the Kawasaki Ki.60, the Messerschmitt Bf 109E and the Shoki, the Nakajima fighter was formally accepted by the J.A.A.F. As production

priority had been awarded the Hayabusa, quantity deliveries of the Shoki did not begin until mid-1942.

Production began with the Ki.44-Ia, or Type 2 Fighter, Model 1a, powered by the 1,250 h.p. Nakajima Ha.41 and carrying an armament of two 7.7-mm. Type 89 and two 12.7-mm. Type 1 machine guns. The Ki.44-Ia attained a maximum speed of 360 m.p.h. at 12,140 ft., attained 9,840 ft. in 3 min. 54 sec., and 16,400 ft. in 5 min. 54 sec., and had a loaded weight of 5,622 lb. By Japanese standards, the wing loading (at 38.4 lb./sq. ft.) was high, and service pilots, unused to the Shoki's high landing speeds and comparative lack of

A Ki.44-Ic Shoki fighter of the type that began to appear in service with the J.A.A.F. in 1943.

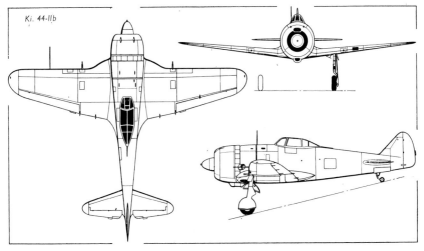

Ki. 44-IIb

manoeuvrability, disliked the new fighter. Only forty Ki.44-Ia fighters were built before the production line switched to the more powerful Ki.44-Ib (Model 1b) with the Nakajima Ha.109 rated at 1,520 h.p. for take-off. This model, which carried four 12.7-mm. machine guns, was succeeded by the Ki.44-Ic with various minor revisions such as modified wheel doors. In 1943 Ki.44-Ib and -Ic Shoki fighters began to appear in all the theatres to which the J.A.A.F. was committed, and initial dislike of the fighter owing to its poor view for take-off and high landing speeds gradually gave place to popularity when the value of its high climb rate and diving speed were appreciated. However, violent snap rolls, high-speed inverted flight, and other manoeuvres were dangerous, and non-combat losses were high.

The Ki.44-IIa (Model 2a) did not enter production, but the modified cockpit canopy, strengthened undercarriage and retractable tailwheel introduced by this model were also featured by the next variant to be manufactured in quantity, the Ki.44-IIb (Model 2b). The Ki.44-IIb Shoki retained the earlier model's four 12.7-mm. gun armament, but the Ki.44-IIc (Model 2c) which was retained largely for the defence of the Japanese home islands replaced two of the 12.7-mm. guns with 40-mm. Ho-301 cannon which proved fairly effective against B-24 Liberator bombers.

Ki.44-Ic Shoki fighters of the J.A.A.F.'s 87th Fighter Squadron.

When B-29 Superfortresses began bombing Japan's industrial centres on northern Kyushu, fighters of this type were sent to the Yamaguchi prefecture in western Japan to intercept these attacks, but the Shoki's most notable success in Japanese skies took place on February 19, 1945, when a small force of these fighters intercepted 120 Superfortresses, destroying 10 of the bombers including two by suicide attacks.

The final production model of the Shoki was the Ki.44-III (Model 3), the loaded weight of which was reduced to 5,357 lb. Its armament comprised two 12.7-mm. and two 20-mm. guns, but relatively few examples of this version had been delivered when Shoki production terminated with the 1,223rd machine.

The following specification relates to the Ki.44-IIb (Type 2 Fighter, Model 2b).

Type: *Single-seat Interceptor Fighter and Fighter-bomber.* **Power Plant:** *One 1,520 h.p. Nakajima Ha.109 fourteen-cylinder radial air-cooled engine.* **Armament:** *Four 12.7-mm. Type 1 machine guns plus two 220-lb. bombs.* **Performance:** *Maximum speed, 376 m.p.h. at 17,060 ft.; cruising speed, 248–273 m.p.h.; range (20 min. reserves), 497 mls. at 13,120 ft.; normal endurance, 2 hr. 20 min.; time to 16,400 ft., 4 min. 17 sec., to 26,250 ft., 9 min. 37 sec.; service ceiling, 36,745 ft.* **Weights:** *Empty, 4,643 lb.; normal loaded, 6,107 lb.* **Dimensions:** *Span, 31 ft. 0 in.; length, 28 ft. 9¾ in.; height, 9 ft. 10⅛ in.; wing area, 161.459 sq. ft.*

NAKAJIMA KI.84 HAYATE (FRANK)   JAPAN

During the summer of 1944 the J.A.A.F. introduced a new warplane, the Ki.84-Ia (Gale) or Type 4 Fighter, Model 1a, which was destined to become for the Allies the most troublesome Army fighter encountered in combat from that time until the end of the war. Employed in all operational theatres, and used for high-, medium-, and low-altitude interception, close-support and dive-bombing, the Hayate differed radically from earlier J.A.A.F. fighters in that relatively light construction gave place to an extremely sturdy structure. It compared favourably with the best of its antagonists; it was slightly slower than the P-51H Mustang and the P-47N Thunderbolt, but it could out-climb and out-manoeuvre both American fighters.

Design work on the Hayate began under the supervision of T. Koyama of the Nakajima Hikoki K.K. in April 1942, and in the re-markably short time of eleven months, the first prototype, powered by a Nakajima Ha.45 Type 4 radial (a J.A.A.F. version of the Navy's NK9A Homare) began flight trials. Quantity production began four months later, in August 1943, at Nakajima's Ota plant, deliveries to the J.A.A.F. commencing in April 1944, and the type entering service during the following August with the 22nd Fighter Squadron based

(Above, right, and below) One of the J.A.A.F.'s best wartime fighters, the Ki.84-**Ia** Hayate.

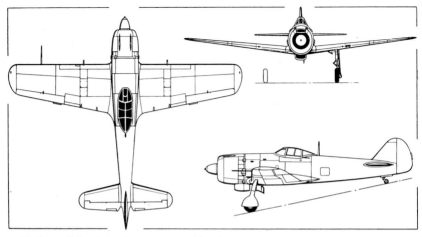

at Hankow, China, being first encountered by General Chennault's 14th Air Force.

The airframe structure of the Hayate followed common Japanese practice of building the centre portion of the fuselage and wing centre section in one piece. The oval-section all-metal fuselage had a flush-riveted stressed-skin, and the wing featured an immensely strong main spar. The first production model, the Ki.84-Ia, carried an armament of two 12.7-mm. machine guns in the forward fuselage decking and two 20-mm. cannon in the wings. In the Ki.84-Ib the machine guns gave place to an additional pair of 20-mm. cannon, while the Ki.84-Ic carried two 20-mm. and two 30-mm. cannon.

From the outset, the Hayate was recognised by the J.A.A.F. as an outstanding design, but

its Ha.45/11 engine was a constant source of trouble. Owing to the extremely compact arrangement of the two rows of cylinders it called for highly skilled maintenance, and oil and fuel pressures had a disconcerting tendency to drop suddenly. The hydraulic system was poorly designed and unreliable, and the legs of the undercarriage tended to snap as a result of poor hardening of the steel employed. In consequence, serviceability was extremely low. Fighters of this type were committed on a large scale for the first time during the decisive battle of Leyte in which the Hayate-equipped 1st, 11th, 22nd, 51st, 52nd, and 200th squadrons participated.

Nakajima's Ota airframe plant had completed twenty-four Hayates by the end of 1943, and in 1944, when the fighter became numeric-

ly the most important in the J.A.A.F., 1,670 machines were produced, a further 992 being completed by the end of the war. Nakajima's Utsonomiya plant, which commenced Hayate production in May 1944, produced 727 machines to bring the grand total manufactured by the parent company to 3,413 aircraft. The Mansyu Hikoki Seizo K.K. (Manchurian Aircraft Manufacturing Company) at Harbin began production of the Hayate early in 1945, delivering a further 100 machines, but plans for the manufacture of the fighter by Tachinawa did not materialise.

Increasing shortages of light alloys led to the investigation of the possibility of employing less critical materials such as wood and steel in the construction of the Hayate. Tachikawa redesigned the entire structure of the Hayate

(Above and below) Ki.84-Ia Hayate fighter-bombers with drop tank under port wing and bomb under starboard wing.

in order to employ wood throughout, and late in 1944 the construction of three prototypes of the wooden Hayate was sub-contracted to Ohji Koku (Prince Aircraft) which, employing largely unskilled labour, built three prototypes at Ebetsu under the designation Ki.106. Apart from some undercarriage redesign and modi-fications to the contours of the vertical ta surfaces, the Ki.106 remained externally simila to the Ki.84, and an excellent finish wa obtained by applying a thick coat of polish t the plywood skin. The first prototype Ki.10 was flown in July 1945 with an Ha.45/21 engine Wooden construction had resulted in some 60

(Above and below) One of the three prototypes of the Ki.106, a wooden version of the Hayate.

lb. increase in normal loaded weight (to 8,598 lb.) which had an adverse effect on manoeuvrability and climb rate (an altitude of 26,240 ft. being attained in 13 min. 5 sec. as compared with 11 min. 40 sec. for the standard Ki.84), but maximum speed compared closely with that of the Ki.84, being 384 m.p.h. at 24,000 ft. The armament of the first prototype was similar to that of the Ki.84-Ib, comprising four 20-mm. cannon, but the second prototype flown on August 13, 1945, carried only two 20-mm. cannon in an effort to conserve weight.

Another attempt to conserve light alloys was the Ki.84-II (Type 4 Fighter, Model 2) built at Nakajima's Ota factory. This had a wooden rear fuselage, wingtips and even control rods, but all-up weight exceeded estimates by a substantial amount, and development was abandoned. Yet another attempt to conserve light alloys was represented by the Ki.113 Steel Hayate which, built by Nakajima, employed steel for as many assemblies as possible, including the cockpit section, the ribs, the bulkheads, etc. Again all-up weight exceeded expectations, causing the abandoning of the project after the completion of one prototype in January 1945.

The Ki.84-III (Type 4 Fighter, Model 3) was fitted with a turbo-supercharged Ha.45ru engine rated at 2,000 h.p., but none had been completed by the end of the war. In an attempt to overcome the difficulties still being experienced with the Ha.45 engine, Mansyu Hikoki took the fourth Ki.84-Ia from its production line at Harbin and adapted the airframe to take a Mitsubishi Ha.112-II fourteen-cylinder radial. Being lighter than the Ha.45, the Ha.112-II demanded lengthened engine mounts in order to maintain the c.g. position, and to compensate for the increased length forward the tail surfaces were enlarged. The Ki.116 weighed about 1,000 lb. less than the Ki.84-Ia with the same armament, but tests were still in progress at the time the Japanese collapsed.

Three further Hayate developments proposed at a design meeting held on June 4, 1945 were the Ki.84R, Ki.84N and Ki.84P. The Ki.84R was to have made use of the improved Ha.45/44 engine which, with a mechanically-driven two-stage three-speed supercharger, was rated at 2,000 h.p. The Ki.84N project, which was assigned the designation Ki.117 for development purposes, was to have had the 2,500 h.p. Nakajima Ha.44/13 (Ha.219) radial and a wing area of 242 sq. ft. The Ki.84P was to have been similar apart from a larger wing of 263.4 sq. ft. area.

The Ki.84 Hayate made an effective dive-bomber, carrying two bombs of from 66-lb. to 550-lb. on detachable underwing racks outboard of the gun ports, and releasing these at 340 m.p.h. at 2,000 ft. During April 1945 Hayate fighter-bombers carried out a series of attacks on U.S. air bases in Okinawa, and during the final months of the war the 10th Flying Division assigned to the defence of Tokyo operated Hayates.

Type: *Single-seat General-purpose Interceptor Fighter and Fighter-bomber.* **Power Plant:** *One 1,900 h.p. Nakajima Ha.45/11 Type 4 eighteen-cylinder radial air-cooled engine.* **Armament:** *Two 12.7-mm. Type 103 machine guns with 350 r.p.g. and two 20-mm. Type 5 cannon with 150 r.p.g., plus max. bomb load of up to 1,100 lb.* **Performance:** *Maximum speed, 388 m.p.h. at 19,680 ft.; maximum cruising speed, 254 m.p.h.; economical cruising, 178 m.p.h.; range (internal fuel), 1,025 mls. at 178 m.p.h., 780 mls. at 254 m.p.h. at 1,500 ft., (max. external fuel) 1,815 mls. at 173 m.p.h.; time to 16,400 ft., 5 min. 54 sec., to 26,240 ft., 11 min. 40 sec.; service ceiling, 34,450 ft.* **Weights:** *Empty, 5,864 lb.; normal loaded, 7,965 lb.; maximum, 9,194 lb.* **Dimensions:** *Span, 36 ft. 10½ in.; length, 32 ft. 6½ in.; height, 11 ft. 1¼ in.; wing area, 226 sq. ft.*

In June 1938, the Japanese Naval Bureau of Aeronautics, recognising the need for a long-range multi-seat escort fighter capable of penetrating deep into enemy territory, approached Mitsubishi and Nakajima with their preliminary requirements. The aircraft, which was intended to fulfil the long-range escort fighter, high-speed reconnaissance and night intruder roles, had to be twin-engined and possess a maximum speed in excess of 320 m.p.h. and normal and maximum ranges of 1,497 and 2,303 miles. The requirements stressed the need for a high standard of manoeuvrability in order that the multi-seat fighter could satisfactorily engage opposing single-engined interceptors.

Although Mitsubishi produced preliminary design studies, owing to a shortage of design personnel, the company was relieved of participation in this 13-*Shi* project for which Nakajima was awarded a development contract under the designation J1N1. The Naka-

jima design team realised from the outset o the project that the size and weight of th aircraft would hinder its manoeuvrability, and therefore made liberal use of leading-edge win slots, trailing-edge flaps and opposite-rotatin airscrews to eliminate the effects of engin torque. The first prototype J1N1 was flow in May 1941. It was a slim, shapely low-win all-metal monoplane with a fixed forward firing armament of one 20-mm. Type 9 cannon and two 7.7-mm. Type 97 machin guns. Its most novel feature was the arrange ment of its rear-firing armament. This com prised four 7.7-mm. guns in a tandem mounted pair of remotely-controlled dorsa barbettes. These barbettes, which were oper ated by the navigator, were considered to complex by the J.N.A.F., and pessimistic pre dictions with regard to the manoeuvrability o such a large aircraft proved well-founded Initial trials were plagued with control diffi culties and the Nakajima engineers found th

(*Below and opposite page, top*) Early J1N1-C-KAI night fighters converted from the J1N1-C.

problems concerning aileron effectiveness impossible of solution. The J1N1 suffered severe aileron vibration during rolls and serious vibration which resulted from buffeting at high angles of attack. Thus, reluctantly, the J.N.A.F. was forced to abandon its concept of a long-range escort fighter.

Despite the J1N1's failure as a fighter, in July 1942 the J.N.A.F. ordered the aircraft into production as the J1N1-C Type 2 Reconnaissance, Model 11. The remotely-controlled gun barbettes were removed as were also the opposite-rotating airscrews, and as a three-seat reconnaissance aircraft the J1N1-C appeared in service over the Solomons in the spring of 1943. Soon after its service début,

(*Below*) *A radar-equipped production J1N1-S Gekko two-seat night fighter.*

the J.N.A.F. found itself in urgent need of effective night fighters to counter marauding B-24 Liberator and B-17 Fortress bombers. Commander Yasuna Kozono of the 251st Air Corps had devised a system of obliquely-mounted armament which was first fitted to converted J1N1-C reconnaissance aircraft to suit them for the night-fighting role. The first recorded successes with these conversions were scored one night in May 1943 when two J1N1-C conversions destroyed two B-24s over Rabaul, New Britain. They mounted two fixed 20-mm. cannon amidships firing forward and upward at an angle of 30° and two firing forward and downward also at an angle of 30°.

A small number of aircraft had been built with a large, dome-like, manually-operated dorsal turret housing a single 20-mm. Type 99 Mk. 1 cannon under the designation J1N1-F, but in August 1943 a variant built from the ground up as a night fighter entered production as the J1N1-S Gekko (Moonlight) Night Fighter, Model 11. The number of crew members was reduced from three to two, and

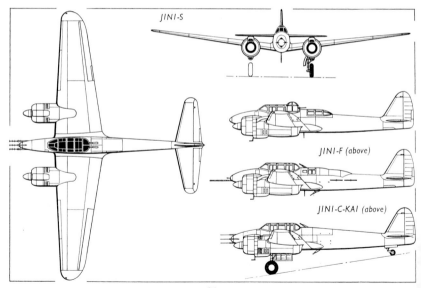

JINI-S

JINI-F (above)

JINI-C-KAI (above)

A J1N1-F three-seat fighter after nosing-over during a landing. Built in small numbers, the J1N1-F had a dorsal turret with a single 20-mm. cannon.

the rear step in the upper line of the fuselage was eliminated. No forward-firing armament was fitted but twin obliquely-mounted 20-mm. cannon were mounted dorsally and ventrally, and some machines carried a small searchlight in the nose. Later production Gekko night fighters were fitted with primitive A.I. radar.

The Gekko enjoyed considerable success during its early operational career. As the war neared the Japanese home islands, Gekko fighters were assigned to the Atsugi base near Yokohama for the night defence of the Kanto and Chubu districts, but they achieved less success against the B-29 Superfortresses. A torpedo-bombing version of the J1N1 was proposed but did not see fruition. Nine proto-

types and 470 production J1N1s were built.

Type: *Two-seat Night Fighter.* **Power Plants:** *Two 1,130 h.p. Nakajima Sakae 21 fourteen-cylinder radial air-cooled engines.* **Armament:** *Four obliquely-mounted 20-mm. Type 99 Model 2 cannon (two dorsal and two ventral).* **Performance:** *Maximum speed, 315 m.p.h. at 19,030 ft., 305 m.p.h. at 10,830 ft.; cruising speed, 207 m.p.h. at 13,120 ft.; time to 9,840 ft., 5 min. 1 sec., to 16,400 ft., 9 min. 35 sec., to 19,685 ft., 11 min. 56 sec.; service ceiling, 30,560 ft.* **Weights:** *Empty, 10,697 lb.; normal loaded, 15,983 lb.; maximum, 17,513 lb.* **Dimensions:** *Span, 55 ft. 8½ in.; length, 39 ft. 11½ in.; height, 13 ft. 1½ in.; wing area, 430.556 sq. ft.*

NAKAJIMA J5N1 TENRAI

The J5N1 Tenrai (Heavenly Thunder) was designed as a potential replacement for the J1N1-S Gekko. Developed under the designation N-20 as a Type B land-based heavy fighter to the 18-*Shi* programme, the Tenrai was initially designed as a single-seater with a heavy forward-firing armament to counter the

B-29 Superfortress bomber which, at that time, had still to make its operational début over Japan.

In the design of the Tenrai, the Nakajima Hikoki K.K. strove to simplify manufacturing processes, the primary aims being a major reduction in the number of components, ease of assembly and the simplification of field maintenance. A low-mid-wing monoplane of clean design and all-metal stressed-skin construction, the Tenrai was powered by two NK9H Homare (Honour) 21 air-cooled radials which, driving four-blade constant-speed airscrews, were rated at 1,990 h.p. for take-off and 1,950 h.p. at 6,400 ft.

(Above, left, and below) Two of the five J5N1 Tenrai heavy interceptor fighter prototypes.

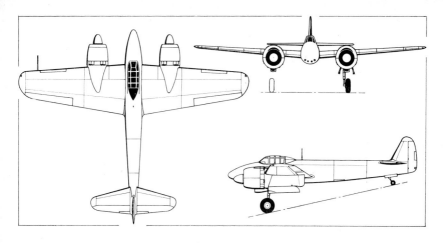

The first prototype J5N1 Tenrai was completed and flown in March 1944, and a further five prototypes were completed, the last two of these being two-seaters. Plans had been prepared for the large-scale subcontracting of Tenrai production, the version intended for service with the J.N.A.F. retaining the single-seat configuration of the first four prototypes. However, the Homare engines failed to develop their rated power, and the fighter was overweight as a result of last-moment demands by the J.N.A.F. for additional armour protection. Test flights revealed that longitudinal stability was bad and the rudder proved ineffective at low air speeds. One of the prototypes crashed while under test. Two more were destroyed by Allied air attacks and, as there seemed little likelihood of rectifying the Tenrai's short-comings without a major redesign, the J.N.A.F. cancelled further development.

Type: *Single-seat Heavy Interceptor Fighter.* **Power Plants:** *Two 1,990 h.p. Nakajima NK9H Homare 21 eighteen-cylinder radial air-cooled engines.* **Armament:** *Two 30-mm. Type 5 cannon and two 20-mm. Type 99 Model 2 cannon.* **Performance:** *Maximum speed, 386 m.p.h. at 20,000 ft., maximum cruising speed, 288 m.p.h.; economical cruising speed, 230 m.p.h. at 9,840 ft.; time to 19,685 ft., 8 min., to 26,250 ft., 11 min.; service ceiling, 35,430 ft.; range (30 min. reserves), 575 mls.; maximum, 920 mls.* **Weights:** *Empty, 11,453 lb.; normal loaded, 15,873 lb.; maximum, 18,078 lb.* **Dimensions:** *Span, 47 ft. 6¾ in.; length, 37 ft. 8¾ in.; height, 11 ft. 5¾ in.; wing area, 344.445 sq. ft.*

With the appearance of the first B-29 Super-fortresses over Japan, the J.A.A.F. was forced to accept the urgency of the need for interceptors with really high-altitude capabilities. At this time Nakajima was already investi-

gating the possibility of a single-seat fighter with an exhaust-driven turbo-supercharger in compliance with an official design study requirement; and the J.A.A.F. instructed the company to proceed with the design and prototype construction with all possible haste.

Allocated the designation Ki.87, the experimental high-altitude interceptor was powered by a Mitsubishi Ha.215 (Ha.44/21) eighteen-cylinder radial rated at 2,400 h.p. for take-off and 1,850 h.p. at 34,450 ft., and cooled by a sixteen-blade fan. The J.A.A.F. wanted the supercharger to be installed in the bottom of the rear fuselage in a similar fashion to that of the P-47 Thunderbolt, but in order to minimize fuel leakage in the event of battle damage, Nakajima preferred to mount the unit on the starboard side of the forward fuselage. The wing was a single-spar stressed-skin unit

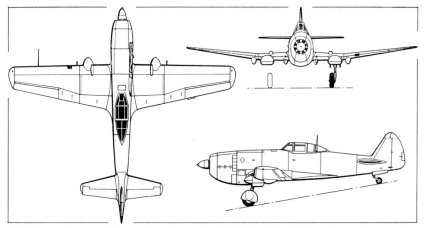

built in one piece, and the oval-section semi-monocoque fuselage was designed to house a light alloy pressure cabin.

In order to conserve space in the inboard wing sections for the 30-mm. ammunition tanks for the Ho-105 cannon mounted outboard of the wheel wells and the 20-mm. ammunition tanks and Ho-5 cannon mounted in the wing roots, the main undercarriage members were arranged to retract rearwards, the wheels turning through 90° to lie flat. Provision was made for a ventral rack carrying a single 550-lb. bomb.

The sole Ki.87-I prototype was flown in April 1945, and plans had been prepared for the production of five hundred machines when the war ended. A further development of the basic design, the Ki.87-II, was on the drawing boards. This was to have been powered by a 3,000 h.p. Ha. 217 engine and the turbo-supercharger was to have been moved to the underside of the rear fuselage. The Ki.87-II had an estimated maximum speed of 461 m.p.h. at 36,000 ft. and a service ceiling of 42,131 ft.

Type: *High-altitude Interceptor Fighter.* **Power Plant:** *One 2,400 h.p. Mitsubishi Ha.215 (Ha.44/21) eighteen-cylinder radial air-cooled engine.* **Armament:** *Two 30-mm. Ho-105 cannon and two 20-mm. Ho-5 cannon.* **Performance:** *Maximum speed (at 12,416 lb.), 438 m.p.h. at 36,090 ft., (at 13,448 lb.), 433 m.p.h. at 36,090 ft.; time to 19,685 ft., 7 min. 44 sec., to 32,810 ft., 14 min. 12 sec.; service ceiling, 42,175 ft.* **Weights:** *Empty, 9,672 lb.; normal loaded, 12,416 lb.; maximum, 13,448 lb.* **Dimensions:** *Span, 44 ft. 0½ in.; length, 38 ft. 4¾ in.; height, 14 ft. 1¼ in.; wing area, 279.862 sq. ft.*

RIKUGUN KI.46-III-KAI (DINAH)   JAPAN

One of the cleanest and most efficient warplanes to see service during the Pacific War was Mitsubishi's Ki.46 Type 100 Command Reconnaissance (Shin-Shitei) monoplane designed by Tomio Kubo. This beautifully contoured monoplane was regarded as the masterpiece of the Japanese aircraft industry, and its excellent performance at altitude made it a thorn in the side of the Allies from the outset of its operational career. In fact, such was the high standard of the Ki.46's design that at one time there was a serious possibility of it being manufactured under licence in Germany for the Luftwaffe. A barter agreement was prepared as part of the Japanese-German Technical Exchange Programme, but negotiations failed to reach fruition.

In March 1943 a faster, more powerful version of the reconnaissance monoplane, the Ki.46-III, made its début. Powered by two 1,500 h.p. Mitsubishi Ha.112-II radials, it attained a maximum speed of 396 m.p.h. at 19,685 ft., and range was 2,485 miles. When

the first B-29 Superfortresses appeared over the Japanese home islands, few of the fighters available to the home-based J.A.A.F. squadrons possessed the high-altitude capabilities necessary for the effective interception of the American bombers. The Rikugun Kokugijutsu Kenkyujo (Army Aerotechnical Research Institute) immediately set up modification lines to turn the Ki.46-III reconnaissance aircraft into the Ki.46-III-KAI Type 100 Air Defence Fighter. The conversion comprised the fitting of a new nose section containing a pair of fixed forward-firing 20-mm. Ho-5 cannon and the installation of a single 37-mm. Ho-203 cannon in the centre fuselage firing forward and upward at an angle of 30°.

The first Ki.46-III-KAI interceptor flew in October 1944, and by the end of November the first aircraft of this type had been delivered to the newly-formed home defence squadrons. A substantial number of Ki.46-IIIs were modified in this fashion by Rikugun until March 1945 when Mitsubishi took over devel-

opment as the Ki.46-IIIb Type 100 Ground Attack, Model 3b. Apart from the obliquely-mounted Ho-203 cannon which was deleted, the Ki.46-IIIb was essentially similar to the Ki.46-III-KAI. It did not progress further than the experimental stage, and the Ki.46-IIIc with modified forward-firing armament never left the drawing-board.

Type: *Two-seat Interceptor Fighter.* **Power Plants:** *Two 1,500 h.p. Mitsubishi Ha.112-II fourteen-cylinder radial air-cooled engines.* **Armament:** *Two 20-mm. Ho-5 cannon and one 37-mm. Ho-203 cannon.* **Performance:** *Maximum speed, 379 m.p.h. at 19,685 ft., 356 m.p.h. at 29,530 ft.; time to 26,250 ft., 20 min. 25 sec.; ceiling, 34,200 ft.* **Weights:** *Empty, 8,446 lb.; loaded, 13,730 lb.* **Dimensions:** *Span, 48 ft. 2¾ in.; length, 37 ft. 7⅞ in.; height, 12 ft. 5½ in.; wing area, 344.445 sq.ft.*

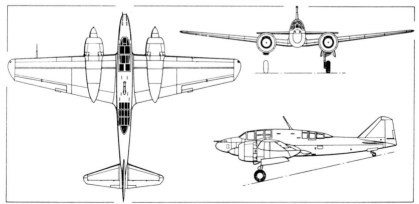

RIKUGUN KI.93   JAPAN

The Ki.93 was the first combat aircraft to be designed entirely by the Army Aerotechnical Research Institute (Rikugun Kokugijutsu Kenkyujo). A two-seat experimental heavy fighter intended for both the bomber destroyer and ground-attack roles, the Ki.93 was first projected late in 1943, and the construction of twelve prototypes was initiated by the 1st Army Air Arsenal (Tachikawa Dai-ichi Rikugun Kokusho), an Army-owned plant which had previously undertook modifications to J.A.A.F. aircraft produced by other manufacturers and had built small quantities of Mitsubishi Ki.30s and also Nakajima Ki.43 Hayabusa fighters.

The Ki.93 was designed specifically to carry a large-calibre cannon in a ventral bulge. It was proposed to install the new 57-mm. Ho-401 cannon in initial production models, combined with a pair of 20-mm. Ho-5 cannon and a flexible 12.7-mm. Ho-103 machine gun, but the use of a 75-mm. field gun was also considered. This gun had been fitted experimentally in a Kawasaki Ki.45-KAId although trials had been unsuccessful, the tail assembly of the aircraft being blown off when the cannon was fired. The Ki.93 was powered by two

The sole prototype of the Ki.93 completed. This aircraft was flown for the first time in April 1945.

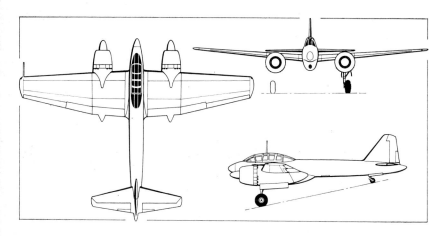

Mitsubishi Ha.214 air-cooled radial engines rated at 1,970 h.p. for take-off and 1,730 h.p. at 27,230 ft. These drove six-blade constant-speed airscrews. The all-metal stressed-skin fuselage was basically of circular section, the two crew members being seated under a curved hood with separate sliding sections. The wing was a two-spar structure and carried large split flaps.

Two variants of the basic design were proposed, the Ki.93-Ia bomber destroyer and the Ki.93-Ib ground-attack fighter which, in addition to the gun armament, carried two 550-lb. bombs on racks between the engine nacelles and fuselage. The first prototype was completed and flown in April 1945 but trials were incomplete at the time of Japan's capitulation. A second prototype was completed with ground-attack armament but no flight trials were made.

Type: *Two-seat Heavy Interceptor and Ground-attack Fighter.* **Power Plants:** *Two 1,970 h.p. Mitsubishi Ha.214 eighteen-cylinder radial air-cooled engines.* **Armament:** *One 57-mm. Ho-401 cannon, two 20-mm. Ho-5 cannon and one flexible 12.7-mm. Ho-103 machine gun plus two 550-lb. bombs.* **Performance:** *Maximum speed, 388 m.p.h. at 27,230 ft.; economical cruising speed, 217 m.p.h.; maximum range (with external fuel), 1,865 mls.; maximum endurance, 6 hr.; time to 9,840 ft., 4 min. 18 sec., to 19,685 ft., 9 min. 3 sec.; service ceiling, 39,535 ft.* **Weights:** *Empty, 16,945 lb.; loaded, 23,514 lb.* **Dimensions:** *Span, 62 ft. 4 in.; length, 46 ft. 7⅞ in.; wing area, 589.323 sq. ft.*

TACHIKAWA KI.94-II   JAPAN

During 1943, as part of a J.A.A.F. investigation of the possibilities of very high altitude pressure-cabin interceptor fighters, the Tachikawa Hikoki K.K. (not to be confused with the Tachikawa Dai-ichi Rikugun Kokusho—1st Army Air Arsenal) was awarded a contract for a design study for such a warplane. The first project, which was allocated the designation Ki.94-I, was a large twin-boom monoplane with two 2,200 h.p. Ha.211ru radials arranged fore and aft of the pilot's pressurised cockpit, the arrangement being generally similar to that adopted some years earlier for the Fokker D.XXIII (see Volume Three). The proposed armament of the Ki.94-I consisted of two 30-mm. Ho-15 and two 37-mm. Ho-203 cannon. Estimated loaded weight was 20,723 lb., and estimated performance included a maximum speed of 485 m.p.h. at 32,800 ft., the ability to attain this altitude in 9 min. 56 sec., and a maximum ceiling of 45,930 ft.

Following an inspection of a full-scale mock-up late in 1943, the J.A.A.F. concluded that the estimated performance figures were unduly optimistic and rejected the design.

Early in the following year the requirement was renewed, but the use of a single engine was now specified. The Tachikawa team therefore produced an entirely new design, the Ki.94-II, which bore a superficial resemblance to the Nakajima Ki.87 which was being developed to fulfil the same requirement. The Ki.94-II was powered by an Ha.219ru (Ha.44/12) air-cooled radial rated at 2,420 h.p. for take-off and 2,042 h.p. at 36,090 ft. This drove a six-blade constant-speed airscrew and the exhaust-driven turbo-supercharger was mounted beneath the pilot's cockpit. The engine employed a cooling fan, and the pilot was accommodated in a light alloy pressure cabin. The wing was of laminar flow section and employed a single main spar, and the mainwheels retracted into the fuselage.

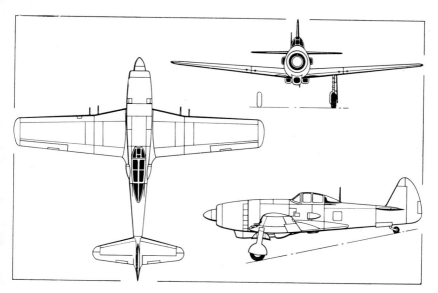

As attacks by B-29 Superfortresses intensified, every effort was made to hurry the completion of the prototype Ki.94-II. This was eventually wheeled out early in August 1945 and the first flight was scheduled for the 18th of that month. This never took place, however, for three days before the scheduled date for the test flight Japan surrendered.

Type: *Single-seat High-altitude Interceptor Fighter.* **Power Plant:** *One 2,420 h.p. Mitsubishi Ha.219ru (Ha.44/12) eighteen-cylinder radial air-cooled engine.* **Armament:** *Two 30-mm. Ho-15 cannon and two 20-mm. Ho-5 cannon.* **Performance** *(Estimated):* *Maximum speed, 302 m.p.h. at sea level, 416 m.p.h. at 32,800 ft., 438 m.p.h. at 39,370 ft.; endurance (30 min. combat at full power), 3.34 hr. at 227 m.p.h. at 13,120 ft., 2.04 hr. at 273 m.p.h. at 29,530 ft.; time to 16,400 ft., 7 min. 50 sec., to 32,810 ft., 17 min. 38 sec., to 39,370 ft., 24 min. 13 sec.; service ceiling, 42,650 ft.* **Weights:** *Empty, 10,339 lb.; normal loaded, 14,110 lb.; maximum, 15,335 lb.* **Dimensions:** *Span, 45 ft. 11⅛ in.; length, 39 ft. 4½ in.; height, 13 ft. 10½ in.; wing area, 301.389 sq. ft.*

DE SCHELDE S.21   NETHERLANDS

The De Schelde S.21 single-seat fighter, designed by T. E. Slot and built by the N.V.Kon.Mij."De Schelde", was never flown, but it warrants inclusion here as, during the war years, it was widely believed to be a new German fighter bearing the designation "Focke-Wulf Fw 198". In fact, no such designation was allocated by the Reichsluftfahrt-ministerium, and the sole prototype of the S.21, which was discovered by the Germans when they occupied the De Schelde factory in May 1940, was transported to Utrecht where it was tested to destruction in the *Zerlege-betrieb* (Analysis Department).

Of extremely unconventional design, the S.21 was intended for the interceptor role and embodied numerous unusual features. Of all-metal construction, it had a reverse-gull wing to which were attached booms carrying the tail assembly. The nose of the fuselage nacelle was extensively glazed and the liquid-cooled DB 600G engine was mounted immediately aft of the cockpit driving a three-blade VDM airscrew by means of an extension shaft. This airscrew could be jettisoned in the event of the pilot having to escape from the aircraft. The radiator was placed under the forward portion of the fuselage nacelle and divided in two by the nosewheel housing.

An exceptionally heavy armament was pro-

*The De Schelde S.21 single-seat interceptor and ground-attack fighter
under construction.*

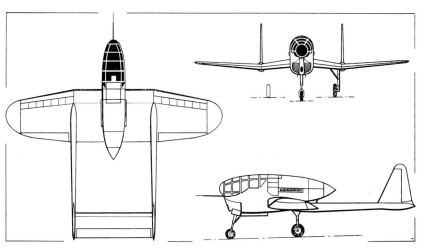

posed for the S.21, this comprising four fixed forward-firing 7.9-mm. machine guns mounted in the sides of the forward fuselage, one flexible 23-mm. Madsen cannon which could also be fixed to fire forward, and one rear-firing 23-mm. cannon firing through the airscrew shaft. The aiming of the latter must have presented some problems, and there is no record of the means by which the designer proposed to overcome these. It was proposed to install a special automatic stabilising system which was intended to permit the pilot to aim the flexible cannon while undertaking ground attack. The wing was fitted with automatic slots, and the instrumentation incorporated a number of innovations, including an airspeed indicator with a diameter of no less than twelve inches!

As no flight testing of the S.21 was undertaken, the figures quoted in the following specification are those of the original design estimates.

Type: *Single-seat Interceptor and Ground-attack Fighter.* **Power Plant:** *One 1,085 h.p. Daimler-Benz DB 600G twelve-cylinder inverted-Vee liquid-cooled engine.* **Armament:** *Four 7.9-mm. FN-Browning machine guns, one flexible 23-mm. Madsen cannon and one fixed, rear-firing 23-mm. Madsen cannon.* **Performance** (*Estimated*): *Maximum speed, 367 m.p.h.; maximum cruising speed, 323 m.p.h.; service ceiling, 33,000 ft.* **Weights:** *Empty, 3,750 lb.; loaded, 5,510 lb.* **Dimensions:** *Span, 29 ft. 6 in.; length, 24 ft. 4¾ in.; height, 8 ft. 6 in.*

FOKKER D.XXI   NETHERLANDS

The D.XXI, designed by Ir. Schatzki to meet the requirements of a specification drawn up by the Royal Netherlands Indies Army, was flown for the first time on March 27, 1936,

powered by a 645 h.p. Bristol Mercury VI-S air-cooled radial. It was an orthodox, sturdy monoplane of simple construction, easily flown and possessing no serious vices. The usual Fokker method of construction was employed. The wing comprised two wooden box spars with plywood ribs and a bakelite-plywood skinning. The ailerons had steel-tube frames with fabric covering, and the fuselage was constructed of welded steel tubes, and from the nose aft to the trailing edges of the wings was covered by detachable metal panels, the rear fuselage being fabric-covered. Unfortunately, shortly after the prototype D.XXI's first flight, defence thinking in the

(Above, left, and below) The prototype D.XXI fighter flown for the first time on March 27, 1936.

One of the thirty-six D.XXI fighters supplied to the Dutch Army Air Service.

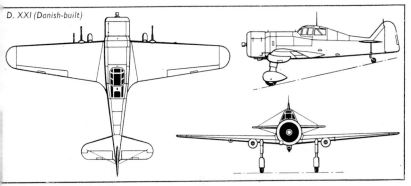

D. XXI (Danish-built)

(*Above*) *One of the first D.XXI fighters built by the Danish Royal Army Aircraft Factory and* (*below, left*) *a close-up view of one of the 20-mm. Madsen cannon carried by the Danish D.XXI.* (*Opposite page*) *Experimental D.XXI with redesigned wing.*

Netherlands Indies underwent a radical change and no orders were placed for the fighter.

In 1937, the Dutch government voted funds for the limited expansion of the *Luchtvaarafdeling* (Army Air Service), resulting in an order for thirty-six D.XXI fighters powered by the 830 h.p. Bristol Mercury VII or VIII. By this time the D.XXI had attracted the attention of several foreign governments and, in 1937, the Finnish government placed an order for seven fighters of this type and acquired a manufacturing licence. Details of Finnish-built D.XXIs appear on pages 12–14 of Volume One. The Spanish Republican government also acquired a manufacturing licence for the

D.XXI, and an initial production batch had reached the assembly stage when the plant building the D.XXIs was overrun by the Nationalist forces, no Spanish-built aircraft flying. The Danish government followed with an order for three D.XXIs and another manufacturing licence. The Danish D.XXIs were powered by the 645 h.p. Mercury VI-S radial and carried a 20-mm. Madsen cannon under each wing. The Royal Army Aircraft Factory at Copenhagen built three D.XXIs in 1939 and a further seven in 1940, and eight of these were in service with No.2 Eskadrille of the Danish Aviation Troops when German forces occupied Denmark.

During the early production life of the D.XXI, Fokker's design office studied numerous developments of the basic design. One machine was flown with a completely redesigned wing which was sharply tapered and had a considerable wash-out towards the tip. Various alternative engines were considered, including the 650 h.p. Rolls-Royce Kestrel V, the 925 h.p. Hispano-Suiza 12Y, and the 750 h.p. Pratt and Whitney Twin Wasp Junior. In 1938, Fokker initiated work on three extensively modified versions of the D.XXI design known by the project numbers 150, 151 and 152. These were to be powered res-pectively by the 1,375 h.p. Bristol Hercules, the 1,050 h.p. Rolls-Royce Merlin, and the 1,090 h.p. Daimler-Benz DB 600H, and featured retractable undercarriages.

When German forces invaded the Netherlands, twenty-nine D.XXI fighters were airworthy. The 1st Fighter Group at De Kooy had eleven D.XXIs on strength, the 2nd Fighter Group at Schipol had ten, and the 5th Fighter Group at Ypenburg had eight. There were many individual heroic exploits by D.XXI pilots, but by the third day of the German invasion the surviving D.XXIs had no ammunition and could not, therefore, participate in the closing stages of the campaign.

Type: *Single-seat Interceptor Fghter.* **Power Plant:** *One 830 h.p. Bristol Mercury VIII nine-cylinder radial air-cooled engine.* **Armament:** *Four 7.9-mm. FN-Browning machine guns with 300 r.p.g.* **Performance:** *Maximum speed, 286 m.p.h.; cruising speed (two-thirds power), 240 m.p.h.; range (at 55% power), 590 mls.; time to 3,280 ft., 1.15 min., to 9,840 ft., 3.4 min., to 19,685 ft., 7.5 min.; service ceiling, 36,100 ft.; absolute ceiling, 37,900 ft.* **Weights:** *Empty, 3,197 lb.; loaded, 4,519 lb.* **Dimensions:** *Span, 36 ft. 1 in.; length, 26 ft. 10¾ in.; height, 9 ft. 8 in.; wing area, 174.375 sq. ft.*

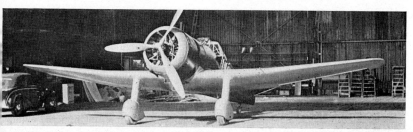

Developed as a private venture, the Fokker G.I was flown for the first time on March 16, 1937, powered by two 750 h.p. Hispano-Suiza 80-02 radial air-cooled engines. These power plants were quickly supplanted by Pratt and Whitney Twin Wasp Junior SB4G radials of similar power, and with a proposed armament of two Madsen cannon and two 7.9-mm.

machine guns firing forward and one flexible 7.9-mm. gun in the tail cone of the fuselage nacelle, plus an 880-lb. bomb load, the G.I aroused a considerable amount of interest. The G.I employed mixed construction, the forward portion of the central nacelle being a metal-covered welded steel-tube structure, the central and rear portions being a wooden monocoque, the wing being a two-spar wooden structure, the forward portions of the booms were of wood and bolted to oval-section metal monocoques, and the tail unit was all-metal, the movable surfaces being fabric-covered.

The Spanish Republican government was the first foreign purchaser of the G.I, the Twin Wasp Junior-powered export model being known as the G.Ib as, in the meantime, the Dutch government had ordered thirty-six examples of an extensively modified variant for the *Luchtvaartafdeling* (Army Air Service)

(Above, left, and below) The first prototype G.I, later rebuilt as a G.Ib for the Spanish government

Six completed G.Ib two-seaters after confiscation by the Netherlands government.

this being known as the G.Ia. Whereas the G.Ib, like the prototype, was a two-seater, the G.Ia was a three-seater, the additional crew member (a radio operator) being housed in the space aft of the pilot which was normally occupied by a fuel tank in the two-seater. The Bristol Mercury VIII radial was specified for the G.Ia, the overall dimensions were increased, and the armament comprised a battery of eight forward-firing 7.9-mm. machine guns with a flexible gun of similar calibre in the tail cone. Deliveries to the *Luchtvaartafdeling* began in 1938, and one G.Ia was experimentally fitted with hydraulically-operated

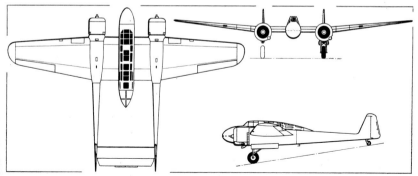

(Above) The first production G.Ia and (below) the 4th machine with an experimental observation cupola.

dive brakes while another was fitted with a glazed observation cupola beneath the fuselage.

The Dutch government placed an embargo on the export of the G.Ia to Spain, and subsequently the Estonian government endeavoured to purchase these aircraft (possibly acting as the agent of the Spanish government), but in the event they were still in the Netherlands at the time of the German invasion, having been confiscated by the Netherlands authorities. All the G.Ib aircraft had been test-flown but owing to the non-delivery of the Madsen cannon none had been fitted with armament at the time of the German attack. Three were hastily fitted with a battery of four machine guns in the nose during the invasion, and saw brief action. When German forces attacked Holland on May 10, 1940, twenty-three G.Ia fighters were at a state of readiness with the 3rd and 4th Fighter Groups of the 1st Air Regiment, but a number of these were des-

(Above) G.Ia fighters of the Army Air Service and (below, left) a G.Ia fitted with experimental dive brakes.

troyed on the ground at Waalhaven and Bergen during the initial Luftwaffe raids. The remainder fought tenaciously until all were destroyed. The surviving G.Ib aircraft and those still on Fokker's assembly line at the time of the occupation were taken over by the Luftwaffe and used as fighter-trainers in Bavaria. These included the machines being built for the Danish government which had been ordered in 1939. The Swedish government had also placed an order for eighteen G.Is which were to be fitted with Swedish Bofors armament.

The following specification relates to the G.Ia, figures quoted in parentheses referring to the G.Ib.

Type: *Three- (Two-) seat Heavy Fighter and Close-support Aircraft.* **Power Plants:** *Two 830 (750) h.p. Bristol Mercury VIII (Pratt and Whitney Twin Wasp Junior SB4G) nine- (fourteen-) cylinder radial air-cooled engines.* **Armament:** *Eight forward-firing 7.9-mm. FN-Browning machine guns and one rear-firing flexible 7.9-mm. gun (two 23-mm. Madsen cannon and two 7.9-mm. FN-Browning machine guns firing forward and one rear-firing flexible 7.9-mm. gun) plus an 880-lb. bomb load.* **Performance:** *Maximum speed, 295 (268) m.p.h.; cruising speed, 221 (199) m.p.h.; range, 945 (913) mls.; time to 9,840 ft., 5.2 (4.95) min., to 19,680 ft., 8.9 (12.1) min.; service ceiling, 30,500 (28,535) ft.* **Weights:** *Empty, 7,326 (6,930) lb.; loaded, 10,560 (10,520) lb.* **Dimensions:** *Span, 56 ft. 3¼ in. (54 ft. 1½ in.); length, 37 ft. 8¾ in. (33 ft. 9½ in.); height, 11 ft. 1¼ in.; wing area, 412.258 (384.27) sq. ft.*

FOKKER D.XXIII

The Fokker D.XXIII single-seat fighter was unique in being powered by two engines which were mounted fore and aft of the pilot's cockpit, driving three-blade tractor and pusher airscrews. The principal design aim was drag reduction, but the power plant arrangement offered several incidental advantages, including the ability to cruise on the power of one engine without serious asymmetrical effects and the increased protection for the pilot provided by the fore and aft engines, eliminating the need for extensive armour protection. The D.XXIII was also the first fighter to have a retractable nosewheel undercarriage.

The prototype was publicly displayed at the 1938 *Salon de l'Aéronautique* in Paris, although the machine had not then been test flown, this event taking place in June 1939 with Gerben Sonderman at the controls. The D.XXIII was

The unique configuration of the D.XXIII held considerable promise, and the proposed Merlin-powered model was expected to attain 385 m.p.h.

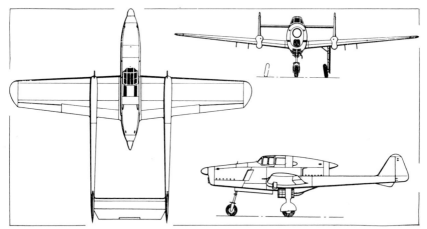

powered by two 540 h.p. Walter Sagitta I-SR twelve-cylinder air-cooled engines, the armament comprising twin 7.9-mm. guns in the fuselage and a 13.2-mm. gun in the root of each boom. Some problems were encountered with the cooling of the rear engine and the feathering of the rear airscrew. Several alternative power plants were considered, including the Junkers Jumo 210G, the Hispano-Suiza Xcrs and the Rolls-Royce Kestrel XV, schemes for the installation of these liquid-cooled engines being drawn up in December 1938, prior to the prototype's first flight, but by the beginning of the Second World War the Rolls-Royce Merlin and the Daimler-Benz DB 601 were under consideration as alternative power plants for the production version, a maximum speed of 385 m.p.h. being anticipated with a pair of either engines. Unfor-

tunately, the sole prototype D.XXIII was riddled with bullets in Fokker's flight test hangar at Schipol during the first Luftwaffe attack of May 10, 1940.

Type: *Single-seat Fighter.* **Power Plants:** *Two 540 h.p. Walter Sagitta I-SR twelve-cylinder inline air-cooled engines.* **Armament:** *Two 7.9-mm. FN-Browning machine guns and two 13.2-mm. FN-Browning machine guns.* **Performance:** *Maximum speed, 326 m.p.h.; cruising speed, 242 m.p.h.; range, 560 mls. at 13,450 ft.; climb to 3,280 ft., 1.35 min., to 16,400 ft., 6.8 min., to 26,240 ft., 16 min.; service ceiling, 29,520 ft.; absolute ceiling, 30,176 ft.; ceiling on one engine, 19,680 ft.* **Weights:** *Empty, 5,060 lb.; loaded, 6,600 lb.* **Dimensions:** *Span, 37 ft. 9 in.; length, 35 ft. 1¼ in.; height, 10 ft. 11¾ in.; wing area, 199 sq. ft.*

KOOLHOVEN F.K.58   NETHERLANDS

The Koolhoven F.K.58 single-seat fighter was completed in 1938, the construction of the first prototype taking only two months from the completion of design work. The F.K.58 employed wooden wings and tail surfaces with plywood skinning, a steel-tube fuselage with metal and fabric covering, and metal-framed, fabric-covered movable control surfaces. The first prototype, which bore the civil reg stration PH-ATO and the constructor's nu mber 5801, was flown for the first time on Septe mber 22, 1938, powered by a 1,080 h.p. His pano-Suiza 14Aa 10 air-cooled radial, attaining a speed of 313 m.p.h. on its init al test flight.

The second prototype (PH-AVA) flew in February 1939 with a similar engine to that installed in the first machine, but prior to this event, on October 10, 1938, the first F.K.58 had been demonstrated before the French authorities at Villacoublay, and, completing its firing trials at Cazaux in the following month, was awarded a contract by the French government. This contract, which called for fifty machines, was placed on behalf of the Ministère des Colonies, the fighters being intended for use in French colonial territories such as Indochina. Two variants were ordered, the F.K.58A with the Gnôme-Rhône 14N/16 fourteen-cylinder radial rated at 1,080 h.p., and the F.K.58 with the Hispano-Suiza 14Aa 10 fourteen-cylinder radial with a similar power rating.

Deliveries to France began on June 17, 1939, and eighteen had been delivered by September 14, 1939. Of these, eleven were Gnôme-Rhône-powered F.K.58As and the remainder were Hispano-Suiza powered. In

The second prototype F.K.58 was flown at the beginning of 1939 and destroyed at Waalhaven in May 1940.

With the Gnôme-Rhône 14N engine the fighter was designated F.K.58A, and eleven aircraft of this type were actually delivered to the Armée de l'Air. The F.K.58A (illustrated above in French insignia) was employed operationally by Patrouilles de Protection in May 1940. (Below) An F.K.58A carrying a Dutch civil registration for ferrying purposes.

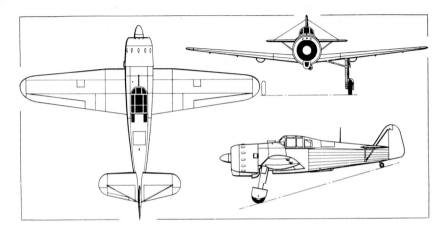

the meantime, in March 1939, the Netherlands government had placed an order for forty F.K.58 fighters powered by the Bristol Taurus engine, and as the N.V. Koolhoven Vliegtuigen had inadequate production capacity, the construction of ten of the French order for F.K.58As was sub-contracted to the Belgian S.A.B.C.A. company. In the event, the Belgian company had completed eight of the airframes with the remaining two in the final stages of assembly at the time of the German invasion of Belgium, but the French government had not delivered any of the Gnôme-Rhône engines.

Apart from the eighteen F.K.58s delivered in June–September 1939, the N.V. Koolhoven Vliegtuigen did not fulfil the French contract, and no aircraft of this type were delivered to the *Luchtvaartafdeling*. The first prototype

crashed at Waalhaven airfield, Rotterdam, on January 4, 1940, and the second prototype was destroyed at Waalhaven by German bombs in May 1940.

Most of the eighteen F.K.58s delivered to France were allocated to *Patrouilles de Protection* in May 1940, their pilots being Polish escapees trained at Lyon-Bron. The Polish pilots found the situation somewhat amusing, commenting that they had "Dutch airframes, French engines, Belgian machine guns, Polish pilots and French skies!" Each *Patrouille* was assigned to the aerial protection of a French town. Four F.K.58s protected Caen, six protected Clermont Ferrand, two protected Salon, and others protected Cognac and La Rochelle. However, there is no record of their subsequent operational activities.

The designer of the F.K.58 fighter, Ir.

112

Schatzki, was, as a former chief designer to the N.V.N.V.Fokker, responsible for the design of the D.XXI, and there were, therefore, a number of features shared by the two fighters. The following specification relates to the F.K.58.

Type: *Single-seat Interceptor Fighter.* **Power Plant:** *One 1,080 h.p. Hispano-Suiza 14Aa 10 fourteen-cylinder radial air-cooled engine.* **Armament:** *Four 7.5-mm. FN-Browning machine guns.* **Performance:** *Maximum speed, 300 m.p.h. at sea level, 313 m.p.h. at 14,760 ft.; cruising speed, 279 m.p.h. at 14,760 ft.; range, 466 mls.; initial climb rate, 2,854 ft./min.; time to 16,400 ft., 6.1 min., to 26,240 ft., 12.2 min.; service ceiling, 34,110 ft.* **Weights:** *Empty, 3,960 lb.; loaded, 5,610 lb.* **Dimensions:** *Span, 36 ft. 1 in.; length, 28 ft. 6½ in.; height, 9 ft. 10 in.; wing area, 185.215 sq. ft.*

The F.K.58 carried its armament of four machine guns in two underwing housings outboard of the undercarriage attachment points. These housings can be seen in the photograph (above) of one of the F.K.58As. (Below) One of the seven Hispano-Suiza-powered F.K.58 fighters prior to delivery to the Armée de l' Air. Most machines ordered under French contract were to have been Gnôme-Rhône powered.

Essentially a progressive development of the P.7, the P.11 fighter was designed by Dipl.-Ing. Pulawski who was killed in a crash on March 21, 1931, six months before the first prototype flew, the subsequent development of the fighter being undertaken by Dipl.-Ing. W. Jakimiuk. The first prototype, the P.11/I, was powered by a Gnôme-Rhône Jupiter, this being followed by the P.11/II powered by a Gnôme-Rhône Mistral, this aircraft being displayed at the *Salon de l'Aéronautique* in Paris in 1932, and the P.11/III with a Gnôme-Rhône-built Mercury IVA.

Production of the fighter as the P.11a began in 1933, the production prototype, the P.11/VI, differing from its predecessors primarily in having an exhaust collector ring combined with a standard Townend cowling ring. Thirty P.11a fighters were delivered to the Polish Air Force in 1934, these being powered by a Skoda-Mercury IV-S2 engine of 500 h.p. and carrying an armament of two 7.7-mm. Browning Mk.33 machine guns with 700 r.p.m. Although, by 1939, most of the P.11a had been relegated to the training schools, several machines actually saw combat during the September campaign.

The P.11b was a variant developed specifically for export and, powered by the 595 h.p. I.A.R.-built Gnôme-Rhône K.9, was ordered by the Rumanian government. Apart from the engine, the geometry of the tail assembly

The P.11c was the principal Polish fighter opposing the Luftwaffe in September 1939.

Fifty P.11b fighters were supplied to Rumania, this type being built subsequently as the P.11f.

differed slightly from that of the P.11a, and fifty were supplied to Rumania before the Industria Aeronautica Romana began the licence manufacture of the type as the P.11f. Four squadrons of the Rumanian Air Force of the 1st Fighter Group "F" based at Bucharest were still equipped with P.11f fighters as late as 1941.

In the meantime, Wsieviod Jakimiuk was further improving the basic design, and towards the end of 1934, the P.11c became the basic production model for the Polish Air Force. The major design change involved the redesign of the forward fuselage in order to improve forward view. This was achieved by lowering the Skoda-Mercury radial, simultaneously raising and moving aft the pilot's seat. The dihedral of the inboard wing sections was increased, a new tail assembly was fitted, and the armament was increased to four 7.7-mm. KM Wz.33 machine guns, the pair in the fuselage sides having 500 r.p.g., and those in the wings having 300 r.p.g. Provision was made for R/T equipment, although this was not installed in all aircraft, and only about one-third of the 175 P.11c fighters produced were fitted with the quartette of guns, delays in the delivery of these necessitating most

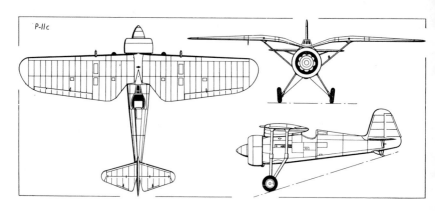

P-llc

aircraft being completed with only two guns.

In the spring of 1939, it was decided to attempt to boost the performance of the P.11 with the object of filling the gap in the re-equipment programme which had resulted from delays in the development of the P.50 Jastrzab. The improved version, designated P.11g and named Kobuz, was to be powered by an 840 h.p. Mercury VIII engine (originally intended for installation in the Jastrzab) driving a larger diameter improved fixed-pitch wooden airscrew, and was to have lengthened undercarriage legs and four of the improved 7.7-mm. KM Wz.36 machine guns. Production of the P.11g Kobuz was initiated at the PWS works in Biala Podlaska in July 1939, and it was anticipated that the first machines would reach the squadrons in the spring of 1940. However, the German invasion interrupted this programme.

The P.11c was popularly known as the *Jedenastka* (the "Eleventh"), and 125 fighters of this type were operational with twelve squadrons of the Polish Air Force during the September campaign.

Type: *Single-seat Interceptor Fighter and Fighter-bomber.* **Power Plant:** *One 645 h.p. PZL-built Bristol Mercury VI S.2 nine-cylinder radial air-cooled engine.* **Armament:** *Two 7.7-mm. KM Wz.33 machine guns with 500 r.p.g. in the fuselage and (some machines) two 7.7-mm. KM Wz.33 guns with 300 r.p.g. in the wings, plus two 27-lb. bombs.* **Performance:** *Maximum speed, 186 m.p.h. at sea level, 242 m.p.h. at 18,000 ft.; range at economical cruising speed, 503 mls., at 155 m.p.h., 435 mls.; time to 16,400 ft., 6 min., to 26,240 ft., 13 min.; service ceiling, 36,080 ft.* **Weights:** *Empty, 2,524 lb.; loaded, 3,960 lb.* **Dimensions:** *Span, 35 ft. 2 in.; length, 24 ft. 9½ in.; height, 9 ft. 4 in.; wing area, 192.7 sq. ft.*

In some respects, the P.24 fighter might be considered as the export equivalent of the Polish Air Force's P.11c as the two fighters were evolved in parallel and embodied a number of common features. The ultimate development of the line of gull-wing fighter monoplanes stemming from Pulawski's P.1 of 1929, the P.24 was stressed to take advantage of radial engines with outputs of up to 1,000 h.p. The first prototype, the P.24/I powered by a 770 h.p. supercharged Gnôme-Rhône 14 Kds fourteen-cylinder two-row radial, was flown in March 1933. Like the P.11c, the engine was lower on the fuselage than that of the original P.11, and the inboard wing sections were revised to improve view from the cockpit. Development of the P.24 was undertaken by the PZL concern as a private venture, and the second prototype, the P.24/II which was used as a demonstration machine for a

number of Balkan air arms, was fitted with an unsupercharged Gnôme-Rhône 14Kfs radial rated at 930 h.p. and driving a three-blade metal airscrew. This prototype was fitted with a pair of 20-mm. Oerlikon FF cannon which were mounted in fairings at the junctions of the wings and bracing struts. In 1934, the PZL chief test pilot, Captain B. Orlinski, established an F.A.I.-recognised speed record of 257.2 m.p.h. The third prototype, which carried a pair of 7.7-mm. machine guns in addition to the twin cannon, was intended to be representative of the proposed production model and was designated P.24A. This also featured a tail assembly similar to that of the P.11c and an enclosed cockpit. The P.24B had an alternative four-gun armament and carried a 220-lb. bomb load.

The first foreign order for the fighter was placed in 1935 by the Turkish government

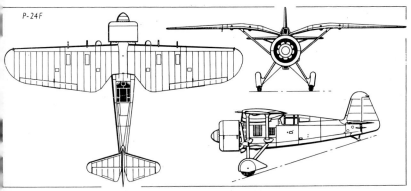

P-24F

117

(Above) The first prototype, the P.24/I and (below, left) the second prototype, the P.24/II.

which ordered forty machines under the designation P.24C, fourteen of these carrying an armament of two cannon and two machine guns and the remainder carrying four machine guns. Structurally, the P.24C differed little from the "A" or "B" variants, but the fairings at the junctions of the bracing struts and the fuselage were omitted. The Turkish government also acquired a manufacturing licence for the P.24C, and the Tayyare Fabrikasi at Kayseri completed its first aircraft on May 27, 1937, limited production continuing under Polish supervision until 1940. Rumania was the next purchaser of the fighter. Designated P.24E, the Rumanian version differed little from the P.24C apart from having an I.A.R.-built Gnôme-Rhône 14 Kmc/36 engine of 930 h.p. and standardising on an armament of two 20-mm. Oerlikon cannon and two 7.7-mm. machine guns. Six airframes were supplied to Rumania by PZL and licence production at the Industria Aeronautica Romana at Brasov (which concern had previously built the P.11f) began in 1937. The P.24E provided the backbone of Rumania's fighter squadrons, and the type was employed on the Russian front.

Bulgaria and Greece ordered batches of P.24 fighters in 1937–38. Bulgaria ordered twenty-four examples of the P.24F with two Oerlikon cannon and two 7.7-mm. machine guns, and Greece ordered thirty P.24Fs and six P.24Gs, the latter having four 7.7-mm. machine guns and no cannon, and carrying two 100-lb. bombs under the wings. Both variants were powered by the 970 h.p. Gnôme-Rhône 14 N7 which was housed in a new low-drag cowling. Two squadrons of the Royal Hellenic Air Force were equipped with the P.24 and operated against the Regia Aeronautica and the Luftwaffe. Until the appearance of such aircraft as the Hurricane, Spitfire, and Messerschmitt Bf 109E, the P.24 was generally considered to be among the most potent fighters extant. It was extremely manoeuvrable and possessed a rugged all-metal structure, but it was approaching obsolescence by the beginning of World War II.

The following specification relates to the P.24F.

(Above) A Turkish P.24C built at Kayseri.

(Above) A P.24G as used by the Royal Hellenic Air Force, and (below) the P.24/II prototype.

Type: *Single-seat Interceptor and Fighter-bomber.* **Power Plant:** *One 970 h.p. Gnôme-Rhône 14 N7 fourteen-cylinder radial air-cooled engine.* **Armament:** *Two 20-mm. Oerlikon FF cannon and two 7.7-mm. machine guns, plus two 55-lb. or 110-lb. bombs.* **Performance:** *Maximum speed, 214 m.p.h. at sea level, 267 m.p.h. at 13,940 ft.; normal range, 497 mls. at 186 m.p.h.; time to 16,400 ft., 5 min. 40 sec., to 26,250 ft., 12 min.; service ceiling, 34,450 ft.* **Weights:** *Empty, 2,924 lb.; loaded, 4,232 lb.* **Dimensions:** *Span, 35 ft. 2 in.; length, 24 ft. 7½ in.; height, 8 ft. 10¼ in.; wing area 192.7 sq. ft.*

119

PZL P.50 JASTRZAB

When, in 1936, a plan was drawn up for the modernisation and expansion of the Polish Air Force, it was foreseen that two types of fighter would be required; a heavy, long-range, two-seat twin-engined destroyer and a light, single-seat, single-engined interceptor. In order to meet the first requirement the PZL P.38 Wilk (Wolf) was designed, this being given priority over the single-seat interceptor, but in the event, the failure of the Foka (Seal) eight-cylinder inverted-Vee engines around which the Wilk had been designed necessitated

An impression of the P.50a Jastrzab prototype which was eventually destroyed by a Polish anti-aircraft battery.

120

the abandoning of the heavy destroyer. The specification for the single-seat fighter was, therefore, revised, calling for a more powerful, heavier machine capable of undertaking some of the roles originally envisaged for the Wilk. To meet the new specification, the PZL design bureau, headed by W. Jakimiuk, evolved the P.50 Jastrzab (Hawk).

The Jastrzab was allocated the highest priority in order to replace the obsolescent P.11, and as the licence production of the Bristol Mercury VIII air-cooled radial was being undertaken by the PZL at Okecie-Paluch, near Warsaw, this engine was selected for installation in the first prototype. With the deterioration of the European situation, the Polish government placed a production order for 300 Jastrzab fighters off the drawing-board, and 150 PZL-built Mercury VIIIs were ordered to power the first half of the order which were to be known as the P.50a. In order to speed the development programme, the British Dowty company was awarded a contract for the design of the Jastrzab's retractable undercarriage which was subsequently to be manufactured by Avia S.A. in Warsaw. It was anticipated that the first Jastrzab prototype would fly in September 1938 with production deliveries commencing a year later, but various delays in the delivery of equipment resulted in the first flight trials taking place five months late, in February 1939.

These trials were not entirely encouraging. The Jastrzab prototype was distinctly underpowered, and even without armament installed its performance fell well below the requirements of the specification. With the Mercury VIII engine its maximum speed was only 280 m.p.h., and maximum range was 466 miles. Manoeuvrability was poor and climb rate inferior. Extensive modifications were made to the airframe, and a Bristol-built Mercury VIII was substituted for the PZL-built engine. Some performance improvements resulted from these changes, but tests with the second prototype Jastrzab, the P.50b with an 870 h.p. Gnôme-Rhône 14 radial, revealed that a substantial increase in power would be necessary in order to exploit the full potentialities of the airframe. PZL had an agreement with the engine division of the Bristol Aeroplane Company permitting the Polish concern to manufacture the full range of Bristol radial engines, and accordingly arrangements to manufacture the 1,375 h.p. Hercules engine for installation in the Jastrzab were accelerated. In the meantime, attempts were made to purchase 1,000 h.p. Pratt and Whitney Twin Wasp radials from the U.S.A. as a stop-gap until the PZL-built Hercules or the new PZL-designed 1,200–1,400 h.p. Waren air-cooled radial became available.

Owing to the disappointing performance of the two Jastrzab prototypes, the production contract was temporarily cut back to thirty machines pending tests of more powerful prototypes, and one hundred and sixty Morane-Saulnier M.S. 406 fighters were ordered from France. A third prototype airframe was prepared for the installation of either the Hercules or the Twin Wasp, whichever power plant came available first. This prototype was subsequently to serve as a test-bed for the PZL Waren, and it was allocated the code-name Kania (Kite). Unfortunately, German forces overran Poland before this aircraft could be completed, and none of the production Jastrzab fighters was flown. An attempt was made to fly the prototype P.50a to Rumania, but the aircraft was brought down by a Polish anti-aircraft battery which mistakenly believed it to be a Luftwaffe machine.

The Jastrzab was of all-metal construction, the three-piece wing carrying Handley Page automatic slots and split trailing-edge flaps, and the fuselage was a semi-monocoque.

The proposed armament for the initial production model comprised four 7.7-mm. machine guns, but later production aircraft were to have had the machine-gun armament supplemented by a pair of 20-mm. cannon and provision for a 660-lb. bomb under the fuselage. With the Hercules radial engine a maximum speed of 348 m.p.h. was anticipated.

The following specification relates to the original P.50a prototype.

Type: *Single-seat Interceptor Fighter.* **Power Plant:** *One PZL-built Bristol Mercury VIII nine-cylinder radial air-cooled engine.* **Armament** (*proposed*): *Four 7.7-mm. KM Wz.36 machine guns and a 660-lb. bomb.* **Performance:** *Maximum speed,* 280 m.p.h.; *range,* 466 mls. *at economical cruising speed.* **Weights:** *Empty* 4,200 lb.; *loaded,* 5,500 lb. **Dimensions:** *Span* 31 ft. 10¼ in.; *length,* 25 ft. 3 in.; *height,* 10 ft 10 in.

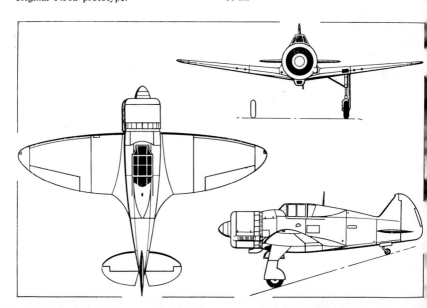

During the Second World War the Rumanian aircraft industry manufactured only one fighter of indigenous design in quantity, the I.A.R.80. This fighter was evolved by the Regia Autonoma Industria Aeronautica Romana of Brasov which, in the mid 'thirties, had produced two low-wing fighter monoplanes of mixed construction, the I.A.R.14 and 15, but had produced only fighters of Polish design in quantity.

In 1937, the I.A.R. concern acquired the manufacturing rights to a modified version of the PZL P-24 single-seat high-wing braced monoplane fighter. Designated P-24E, the fighter was powered by an I.A.R.-built Gnôme-Rhône 14K Mistral-Major fourteen-cylinder radial air-cooled engine rated at 940 h.p. for take-off, and carried an armament of two 7.7-mm. machine guns and two 20-mm. Oerlikon FF cannon. Six P-24E airframes were acquired from Poland to serve as prototypes, and while preparations for the quantity manufacture of this fighter were being made on behalf of the Rumanian Air Force, the I.A.R. design department, headed by Eng. Mircea Grossu-Viziru, began the development of a further fighter of original design, the I.A.R.80. The new fighter employed the stressed-skin duralumin rear fuselage, tail surfaces, the engine, engine mount and cowling, and various other components of the P-24E married to new forward and centre fuselage sections, and a new wing.

The prototype I.A.R.80 appeared late in 1938, but production of the fighter did not commence until 1941, this type supplanting the P-24E on the assembly line at Brasov. The production model differed from the prototype in having a sliding cockpit canopy, slightly modified tail surfaces, and the original wing-mounted armament of four 7.7-mm. machine guns supplemented by a pair of 20-mm. cannon, early production machines having MG FF (Oerlikon) cannon and later machines having Mauser MG 151s. Underwing racks were provided for two 110-lb. or 220-lb. bombs.

Rumanian home defence squadrons began to receive the I.A.R.80 early in 1942, and production continued until the beginning of 1943 when the Brasov plant began to re-tool for the production of the Messerschmitt Bf 109G. Between January and April 1944, approximately 120 I.A.R.80 fighters were defending Rumanian airfields. A very small number of a modified version, the I.A.R.81, were produced before production gave place to the Bf 109G. This model had a ventral bomb rack for a single 440-lb. bomb. Two 110-lb. bombs could also be carried underwing.

Type: *Single-seat Interceptor Fighter and Fighter-bomber.* **Power Plant:** *One 940 h.p. I.A.R.-built Gnôme-Rhône 14K Mistral-Major fourteen-cylinder radial air-cooled engine.* **Armament:** *Four 7.7-mm. machine guns and two 20-mm. cannon plus two 220-lb. bombs.* **Performance:** *Maximum speed, 317 m.p.h. at 13,000 ft.; maximum range, 590 mls.; climb to 16,400 ft., 6 min.; service ceiling, 34,500 ft.* **Weights:** *Empty, 3,930 lb.; normal loaded, 5,040 lb.; maximum, 5,480 lb.* **Dimensions:** *Span, 32 ft. 10 in.; length, 26 ft. 9½ in.; height, 11 ft. 10 in.; wing area, 167 sq. ft.*

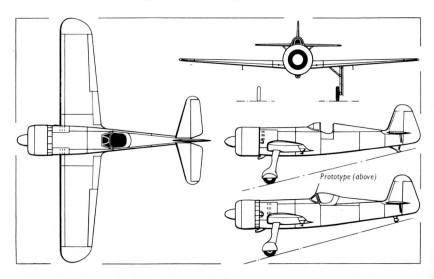

Prototype (above)

BEREZNIAK-ISAEV BI-1   SOVIET UNION

From the early 'thirties several Soviet engineers manifested interest in the use of rockets both as a primary power plant and as a means of boosting the performance of piston-engined aircraft. The first attempt to boost fighter performance by means of small auxiliary rockets took place in 1934–35 with a Tupolev I-4 which was fitted with six small solid-fuel rockets. Research was intensified as war approached, and during 1939–40 design work was initiated on several rocket-propelled short-range target-defence interceptors.

Three aircraft were produced as part of the rocket fighter programme, the Tikhonravov 302, a design by N. N. Polikarpov dubbed the *Malyutka* (Little One), and the BI-1 designed by engineers Berezniak and Isaev under the supervision of V. F. Bolkhovitnov. All three fighters were powered by a single 1,100 lb. thrust Dushkin bi-fuel rocket motor. The

three types underwent powered trials in 1942, but only the BI-1 was proceeded with, and no details of the Tikhonravov 302 or *Malyutka* were subsequently revealed.

In July 1941, the BI-1 design was submitted to the Defence Committee (which comprised five members: Stalin, Beria, Kaganovich, Molotov and Malenkov), and approval was given for the immediate construction of a pre-series of five aircraft. The BI-1 was a low-wing cantilever monoplane of simple mixed construction which was designed to facilitate mass production. The undercarriage comprised inward-retracting main members and a small tail skid, the armament and radio equipment were mounted in the fuselage nose and immediately aft of the pilot's cockpit respectively, and the fuel tanks, pumps and rocket motor were housed in the rear fuselage.

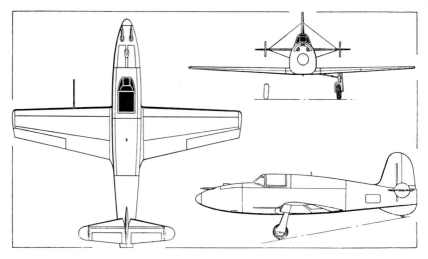

The BI-1 was flown as a glider for the first time on September 10, 1941, being towed into the air behind a twin-engined Pe-2 bomber. Trials were undertaken by two pilots, K. Gruzdev and G. Bakhchivandii, and the latter made the first powered flight with the BI-1 on May 15, 1942. The Dushkin rocket gave the BI-1 a powered flight endurance of eight to fifteen minutes, but this was considered insufficient for operational purposes, and therefore a multi-chamber rocket motor was evolved, one chamber providing 20–30 per cent thrust for cruising and the others providing 70–80 per cent thrust for combat. However, the new motor proved to be somewhat erratic under test, the fuel system was rather complex and its weight was more than twice that of the original single-chamber power plant. By this time, the VVS-RKKA and the PVO were demanding fighters with a good endurance, and the requirement for a short-range target-defence interceptor was cancelled.

Type: *Single-seat Target-defence Interceptor.* **Power Plant:** *One 1,100 lb. Dushkin bi-fuel liquid rocket motor.* **Armament:** *Two 20-mm. ShVAK cannon.* **Performance:** *Powered endurance, 8–15 min. No further details available for publication.* **Weights:** *No details available.* **Dimensions:** *Span, 23 ft. 7½ in.; length, 22 ft. 11½ in.; height, 6 ft. 10¾ in.*

126

LAVOCHKIN LAGG-3

The fighters stemming from the design bureau headed by Semyon Alexse'evich Lavochkin, together with those of Alexander Yakovlev did much to turn the tide of the air war over the Eastern Front in favour of the VVS-RKKA. Lavochkin and his contemporary, Yakovlev, both produced fighters to meet the 1938 programme, but that of Lavochkin, initially designated I-22, was the first to fly, the maiden flight of the first prototype taking place on March 30, 1939. Later, when the system of designating Soviet military aircraft was changed from that in which the letter "I" (indicating *Istrebitel*, or Fighter) was followed by a number to one in which an indication of the design bureau took the place of the function letter, the fighter received the designation LaGG-1. This indicated that the principal designer, Lavochkin, was assisted

by engineers Gorbunov and Gudkov, and that it was the first fighter design (odd numbers being applied to fighters and even numbers to other types).

Production of the LaGG-1 began in 1940, but prior to the commencement of deliveries to the VVS-RKKA, a number of changes were made, primarily aimed at improving controllability and increasing structural strength. A modified prototype was flown under the designation I-301, and with the modifications introduced on the production line, deliveries began early in 1941 as the LaGG-3. The fuselage of the LaGG-3 was built up on Siberian birch frames with a plywood skin impregnated with phenol-formaldehyde, the fin was integral with the fuselage, the wings were two-spar wooden structures, and all control surfaces were metal-framed and fabric-covered. The undercarriage

(Above) A LaGG-3 captured by the Finns. Note bulge on starboard side of engine cowling. (Below, left) An early LaGG-3 tested by the Japanese.

was fully retractable, the main members retracting hydraulically upwards and inwards into the wings and the tailwheel retracting backwards. Five fuel tanks were provided, three in the centre section and one in each outer section of the wings, total fuel capacity being 105.6 Imp. gal., and the M-105P (the suffix "P" indicating *Pushka*, or Cannon) engine drove a VISh-61P three-blade metal airscrew. Various armament combinations were installed in the production LaGG-3, these including the following: (1) One 20-mm. ShVAK cannon with 120 rounds, one 12.7-mm. Beresin BS machine gun with 220 rounds, and one 7.62-mm. ShKAS with 325 rounds; (2) the same but with an additional ShKAS gun; (3) One 23-mm. VIa cannon and 80 rounds plus two ShKAS and one BS machine gun; (4) Three BS and two ShKAS machine guns; (5) One ShVAK cannon and two BS machine guns, and (6) One ShVAK cannon and one BS machine gun. The variant with the five-gun armament was normally used as an escort for Il-2 assault aircraft, and carried two 22 Imp. gal. long-range tanks.

Finnish pilots who tested a captured LaGG-3 fighter were somewhat critical of the aircraft's qualities, expressing the opinion that, although superior to the MiG-3, the LaGG-3 had poor acceleration and tended to spin in sharp turns. The Japanese also evaluated a LaGG-3 in 1942 when a political refugee flew

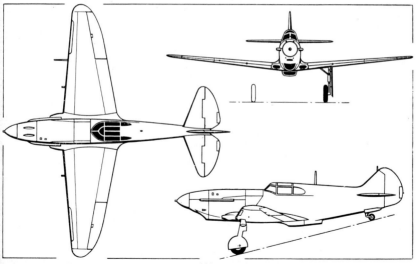

This LaGG-3, photographed at Mutanchiang, was delivered to the Japanese by a Russian deserter in the Spring of 1942.

a fighter of this type to Manchuria. Whereas the Finnish pilots had deplored the LaGG-3's acceleration, Japanese test pilots considered its acceleration and high diving speeds to be its most outstanding qualities, although, by Japanese standards, manoeuvrability was extremely poor. It was universally agreed, however, that the Russian fighter possessed an extraordinarily robust structure, and structural weight was outstandingly low. By the beginning of 1942, the LaGG-3 was numerically the most important fighter serving with the VVS-RKKA, continuing in production until the summer of 1942 when it was finally supplanted on the assembly lines by the radial-engined La-5.

Type: *Single-seat Interceptor and Fighter-bomber.* **Power Plant:** *One* 1,100 *h.p. Klimov* *M-105P (VK-105P) twelve-cylinder Vee liquid-cooled engine.* **Armament:** *One* 20-mm. ShVAK *cannon with* 120 *rounds, one* 12.7-mm. Beresin BS *machine gun with* 220 *rounds, and two* 7.62-mm. ShKAS *machine guns with* 325 *r.p.g., plus six* RS-82 *rocket missiles or two* 220-lb. *and two* 22-lb. *bombs, two* 110-lb. *and two* 55-lb. *bombs, or two* 110-lb. *bombs and four* 55-lb. *bombs.* **Performance:** *Maximum speed (at* 7,032 *lb.),* 348 *m.p.h. at* 16,400 *ft.; cruising speed,* 280 *m.p.h.; range (internal fuel),* 404 *mls., (with two* 22 Imp. gal. *auxiliary tanks)* 497 *mls.; endurance,* 1 *hr.* 53 *min.; time to* 9,840 *ft.,* 3 *min.* 4 *sec., to* 16,400 *ft.,* 7 *min.* 6 *sec., to* 26,250 *ft.,* 19 *min.* 12 *sec.; ceiling,* 29,530 *ft.* **Weights:** *Empty,* 5,776 *lb.; normal loaded,* 7,032 *lb.; maximum,* 7,230 *lb.* **Dimensions:** *Span,* 32 *ft.* 1¾ *in.; length,* 29 *ft.* 1¼ *in.; height,* 8 *ft.* 10 *in.; wing area,* 188.5 *sq. ft.*

LAVOCHKIN LA-5

Late in 1941, Semyon Lavochkin adapted a LaGG-3 airframe to take a Shvetsov M-82A two-row fourteen-cylinder radial air-cooled engine in place of the liquid-cooled inline Klimov M-105P. The modified aircraft was flown for the first time at the beginning of 1942, and during the course of trials displayed a maximum speed some 25 m.p.h. superior to that of the Messerschmitt Bf 109F at low altitudes. The VVS-RKKA required a fast-climbing, highly manoeuvrable low-altitude interceptor, and the modified LaGG-3 fulfilled this requirement admirably. Later, in combat, it was rarely operated much above 16,000 feet, and close to the ground it was at its best, many Luftwaffe fighters stalling and crashing when attempting to follow it in a tight turn.

Designated La-5, the radial-engined fighter immediately supplanted the LaGG-3 on the assembly lines. In fact, the first series of La-5s were modified LaGG-3 airframes, but at an early stage in the production programme the rear fuselage was cut down and an all-round-vision cockpit canopy provided. Armament comprised two 20-mm. ShVAK cannon mounted in the forward fuselage above the engine, and the structure was identical to that of the LaGG-3; the fuselage being built on birch frames with plywood skinning, the wings being two-spar wooden structures, and the movable control surfaces being metal-framed and fabric-covered. All undercarriage members were hydraulically retractable. The La-5 made its operational début during the autumn operations in the area of Stalingrad which marked the turning point in the war insofar as the VVS-RKKA was concerned. It attained a maximum speed of 373 m.p.h. at sea level and 355 m.p.h. at 16,400 ft., and proved particularly effective as a close-support weapon.

By 1943, an improved model was beginning

The early production La-5 (below) did not have the all-round-vision cockpit canopy later introduced on the production line.

(Above and below) The La-5 made its operational début in the Stalingrad area in 1942.

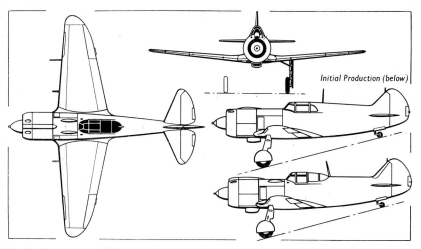

Initial Production (below)

(Right) The more powerful La-5FN introduced in 1943.

to reach the operational squadrons, the La-5FN, the "FN" suffix indicating *Forsirovannii Neposredstvennim*, or Boosted Engine. The M-82FN (ASh-82FN) engine employed direct fuel injection which boosted maximum output from 1,600 h.p. to 1,640 h.p. and offered a nominal maximum output of 1,430 h.p. at 16,400 ft. Mixed construction was introduced, the wooden longerons being replaced by metal longerons, internal fuel capacity was increased to 116.5 Imp. gal., the undercarriage was lightened, and the controls were improved. The principal external differences between the original La-5 and the La-5FN was the intake

The La-5FN was flown by many of the leading Russian aces. Its engine employed direct fuel injection which boosted maximum output from 1,600 h.p. to 1,640 h.p.

over the engine which, in the later model, was brought forward to the front of the cowling. The La-5FN appeared in large numbers during the Battle of Kursk, and was flown by many

The La-5FN had a rugged, wooden structure.

of the leading Russian aces. Although the La-5FN was not so technically complete as its foreign contemporaries it compared favourably in other respects, possessed a rugged structure, was easily maintained under operational conditions, was light and was simple to build.

The following specification relates to the La-5FN.

Type: *Single-seat Interceptor and Fighter-bomber.* **Power Plant:** *One 1,640 h.p. Shvetsov M-82FN (ASh-82FN) fourteen-cylinder radial air-cooled engine.* **Armament:** *Two 20-mm. ShVAK cannon with 200 r.p.g., plus a 330-lb. bomb load.* **Performance:** *Maximum speed, 402 m.p.h. at sea level, 386 m.p.h. at 16,400 ft.; time to 16,400 ft., 4.7 min.* **Weights:** *Loaded, 7,406 lb.* **Dimensions:** *Span, 32 ft. 1¾ in.; length, 27 ft. 10¾ in.; height, 9 ft. 3 in.; wing area, 188.5 sq. ft.*

LAVOCHKIN LA-7

Progressive development of the basic La-5FN design led, in 1943, to the La-7 which, during the closing stages of the war in Europe, was flying with a substantial proportion of the VVS-RKKA fighter squadrons operating on the Eastern Front, and was flown by many of the leading pilots, including Russia's top aces, Ivan Kojedub and Alexander Pokryshin with 62 and 59 victories respectively.

The La-7 was essentially a refined, more powerful and more effectively armed version of the La-5FN. The fourteen-cylinder Shvet-sov M-82FN radial was boosted to 1,775 h.p. for take-off, the armament was increased to three 20-mm. ShVAK cannon in the forward fuselage over the engine, two mounted to port and one mounted to starboard, and the engine cowling was generally cleaned up, the intake over the cowling being eliminated and the oil coolant radiator being moved aft to a position under the cockpit. The structure of the La-7 was identical to that of the La-5FN.

During 1944 attempts were made to improve the performance of the La-7 for short periods

This La-7 fighter was flown by one of Russia's leading aces, Ivan Kojedub, who gained the last of his 62 victories with this machine.

A tandem two-seat version of the basic La-7, the La-7U (above) was introduced in 1944 for the high-speed liaison and reconnaissance roles and for conversion training. The La-7 on the opposite page was supplied to the Czechs.

by installing a liquid-fuel rocket motor in the extreme rear fuselage. This rocket motor, the power of which has never been revealed, boosted maximum speed by ten to fifteen per cent for brief periods, and was considered sufficiently reliable to permit its service introduction on a small scale, although it is believed that La-7s so equipped were confined to the units of the PVO (*Protivovozdushnoi Oborony*, or Protective Air Force).

A further variant of the basic La-7 was the tandem two-seat La-7U which, appearing in 1944, was used for the high-speed liaison and reconnaissance roles as well as conversion training. The two occupants were enclosed by a continuous cockpit canopy with separate sliding sections, and the tail surfaces were

enlarged. The oil coolant radiator reverted to the position that it held on the La-5FN. Relatively few La-7Us were built.

Type: Single-seat Interceptor and Fighter-bomber. **Power Plant:** *One 1,775 h.p. Shvetsov M-82FN (ASh-82FN) fourteen-cylinder radial air-cooled engine.* **Armament:** *Three 20-mm. ShVAK cannon plus six RS-82 rocket missiles or two 110-lb. or 220-lb. bombs.* **Performance:** *Maximum speed, 413 m.p.h. at sea level, 395 m.p.h. at 16,400 ft., (with auxiliary rocket motor) 430 m.p.h. at 16,400 ft.; time to 16,400 ft., 4.2 min.; ceiling, 33,300 ft.* **Weights:** *Loaded, 7,495 lb.* **Dimensions:** *Span, 32 ft. 1¾ in.; length, 27 ft. 10½ in.; height, 9 ft. 2 in.; wing area, 188.5 sq. ft.*

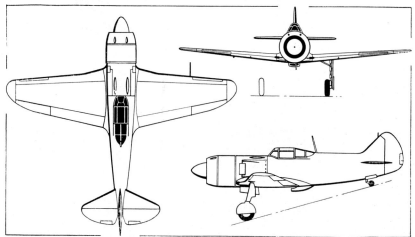

The final wartime development of the series of single-seat fighters designed by Semyon Lavochkin's bureau and stemming from the LaGG-1 of 1939 was the La-9. Although the La-9 bore a close external similarity to the earlier La-7, it was structurally a radically different aircraft. An extremely compact aeroplane with aerodynamically clean lines, the La-9 was of all-metal, stressed-skin construction. The two-spar, all-metal wing was completely redesigned, the leading edge being brought forward from a point just outboard of the undercarriage attachment points and the tips being clipped. Split trailing edge flaps were fitted inboard of the ailerons, these being metal-framed and fabric-covered. The tailplane, like the wing, featured square-cut tips, but unlike the La-7, the rear fuselage was not cut down aft of the cockpit, resulting in a somewhat restricted rear view for the pilot. The asymmetrical arrangement of three cannon was discarded in favour of four cannon arranged symmetrically, the breeches necessitating bulges in the panelling forward of the cockpit.

Deliveries of the La-9 to the VVS-RKKA commenced shortly before the cessation of hostilities, and it is improbable that the fighter saw more than isolated action. Various means of boosting the performance of the La-9 were investigated simultaneously with the service introduction of the fighter. Prior to the end of 1944, the La-9 had been tested with two liquid-fuel rocket motors mounted under the wings, with two ramjets, and with two impulse ducts similar to that employed by the German Fieseler Fi 103 missile. Shortly after the war, on August 18, 1946, several rocket-boosted La-9 fighters were demonstrated over Tushino, together with a formation of La-9s each equipped with a pair of impulse ducts.

A further development of the design, the La-11, flew in 1946, and was standard equipment with many VVS-SA (successor to the VVS-RKKA) regiments during the immediate post-war years.

Two La-9s each fitted with a pair of impulse ducts (pulsating athodyds) intended to boost the fighter's performance. Trials were undertaken late in the war.

Type: *Single-seat Interceptor and Escort Fighter.* **Power Plant:** *One 1,870 h.p. Shvetsov ASh-82FNV fourteen-cylinder radial air-cooled engine.* **Armament:** *Four 20-mm. ShVAK cannon.* **Performance:** *Maximum speed, 428 m.p.h. at sea level, 405 m.p.h. at 11,480 ft.; cruising speed, 312 m.p.h.; initial climb rate, 3,840 ft./min.; time to 16,400 ft., 4.2 min.; service ceiling, 36,500 ft.* **Weights:** *No details available for publication.* **Dimensions:** *Span, 34 ft. 9¼ in.; length, 30 ft. 2¼ in.; height, 9 ft. 8 in.*

An impression of one of the La-9 fighters supplied to the Sino-Communist government.

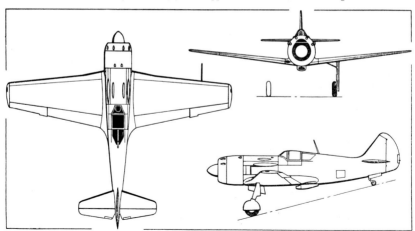

MIKOYAN-GUREVICH MIG-1   SOVIET UNION

The first result of the collaboration of designers Artem I. Mikoyan and Mikhail I. Gurevich, the MiG-1 single-seat fighter introduced an element of modernity into the Russian fighter scene with its service appearance in 1941. Although the MiG-1 could not claim the distinction of being the first low-wing cantilever monoplane with a liquid-cooled

engine and a retractable undercarriage to enter service with the VVS-RKKA, this having gone to Polikarpov's I-17, it was the first of Russia's wartime generation of fighters.

Designed as part of the same programme which resulted in the Yak-1 and LaGG-1, the first prototype MiG-1 was flown in March 1940 under the designation I-61, the design and construction of the fighter having taken little more than three months! During its first flight trials, the I-61 alias MiG-1 attained a speed of 373 m.p.h. at 22,970 ft., and quantity production of the fighter was started immediately. The MiG-1 was of mixed construction, the wing outer panels, the rear fuselage and tail assembly being of wood, and the wing centre section, forward fuselage and control surfaces being of metal. The Mikulin AM-35 liquid-cooled engine drove a three-

(Above left and below) The MiG-1, first flown in March 1940, was originally designated I-61. A total of 2,100 was built.

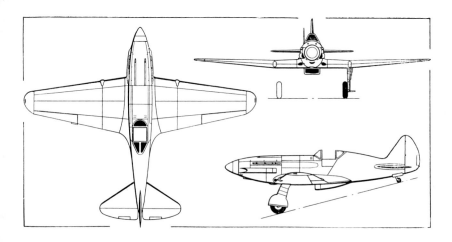

blade metal constant-speed VISh-22E, -22D-3 or -22M airscrew, and the 88 Imp. gal. of fuel was housed in two tanks in the wing centre section and a third tank immediately aft of the engine. The only armour protection for the pilot comprised a 9-mm seat plate.

The hurried development of the MiG-1 rendered itself apparent in the flying characteristics of the fighter. The extremely short fuselage resulted in poor longitudinal stability, and take-offs and landings were extremely delicate operations, the fighter tending to swing severely unless extreme care was taken by its pilot. Two thousand one hundred MiG-1 fighters were completed and delivered to the VVS-RKKA and PVO before the type was supplanted on the assembly lines by the improved MiG-3 in 1941.

Type: *Single-seat Interceptor and Fighter-bomber.* **Power Plant:** *One 1,200 h.p. Mikulin AM-35 twelve-cylinder Vee liquid-cooled engine.* **Armament:** *Two 7.62-mm. ShKAS machine guns with 375 r.p.g. and one 12.7-mm. Beresin BS machine gun with 300 rounds, plus six RS-82 rocket missiles, or two 220-lb. or 110-lb. bombs, or four 55-lb. bombs, or two VAP-6M or ZAP-6 chemical containers.* **Performance:** *Maximum speed, 390 m.p.h. at 22,965 ft.; normal cruising speed, 280 m.p.h.; maximum range (at 70% power and a reserve of 9 Imp. gal.), 360 mls. at 342 m.p.h.; time to 16,400 ft., 5.3 min.; ceiling, 39,370 ft.* **Weights:** *Empty, 5,721 lb.; normal loaded, 6,834 lb.; maximum, 7,290 lb.* **Dimensions:** *Span, 33 ft. 9½ in.; length, 26 ft. 8¾ in.; height, 8 ft. 6 in.; wing area, 189.44 sq. ft.*

MIKOYAN-GUREVICH MIG-3   SOVIET UNION

A progressive development of the MiG-1, the MiG-3, initially designated I-200, was flown for the first time in 1941, earning a Stalin Prize for its designers. The most important difference between the MiG-1 and MiG-3 was the power plant of the latter which was the more powerful AM-35A which drove a VISh-61Sh airscrew. In order to improve range, a supplementary fuel tank containing 52 Imp. gal. was mounted beneath the pilot's seat, and dihedral on the outboard wing panels was increased to improve stability. The pilot's cockpit was fitted with a sliding canopy, and the fuselage aft of the cockpit was cut down at an angle and glazed in order to improve rear vision. The hinged lower halves of the under-carriage cowlings were detached from the legs and attached to the fuselage, and the ventral

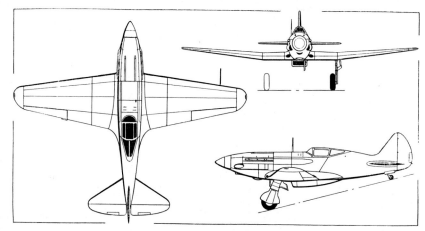

radiator bath was enlarged and extended forward.

The MiG-3 began to appear in service late in 1941, and it was while flying a fighter of this type that one of the VVS-RKKA pilots, later to become an ace, Guards-Colonel A. Pokryshkin, discovered Von Kleist's panzer forces which were threatening Rostov-on-Don. Several thousand MiG-3 fighters were produced but, although fast, their manoeuvrability was relatively poor and their armament was inadequate by contemporary standards. They were thus at a distinct disadvantage when opposing Luftwaffe fighters, and with the availability of superior fighters, such as the Yak-1, the MiG-3 was progressively relegated to the high-speed tactical reconnaissance role, and by the end of 1943 the type had virtually disappeared from the first-line units of the VVS-RKKA and PVO engaged on Russia's western front.

Type: *Single-seat Interceptor and Fighter-bomber.* **Power Plant:** *One* 1,350 *h.p. Mikulin AM-35A twelve-cylinder Vee liquid-cooled engine.* **Armament:** *Two* 7.62-*mm. ShKAS machine guns with* 375 *r.p.g. and one* 12.7-*mm. Beresin BS machine gun with* 300 *rounds, plus six RS-82 rocket missiles, or two* 220-*lb. or* 110-*lb. bombs, or four* 55-*lb. bombs, or two VAP-6M or ZAP-6 chemical containers.* **Performance:** *Maximum speed,* 407 *m.p.h. at* 22,965 *ft.; range,* 510 *mls. at* 342 *m.p.h.; time to* 16,400 *ft.,* 4.5 *min.; ceiling,* 39,370 *ft.* **Weights:** *Normal loaded,* 7,242 *lb.; maximum,* 7,695 *lb.* **Dimensions:** *Span,* 33 *ft.* 9½ *in.; length,* 26 *ft.* 8¾ *in.; height,* 8 *ft.* 7 *in.; wing area,* 189.44 *sq. ft.*

143

MIKOYAN-GUREVICH MIG-5

SOVIET UNION

Some mystery surrounds the MiG-5 single-seat fighter, the designation having been credited to a radial-engined development of the MiG-3 which was in service with the VVS-RKKA in small numbers in 1943, and to a twin-engined single-seat fighter, evidence for the existence of which is confined to a British wartime intelligence report. No Russian source has ever made reference to this twin-engined fighter which, according to the report, was powered by twin Klimov VK-105 liquid-cooled engines, carried an armament of two 20-mm. ShVAK cannon, one 12.7-mm. BS machine gun and two 7.62-mm. ShKAS machine guns firing forward and a fixed rear-firing 12.7-mm. BS gun, and had a retractable nosewheel undercarriage. It is likely, however, that this machine was, in fact, the SAM-13 which, designed by a team headed by Alexander Moskalov, was flown for the first time in 1941. This aircraft, the prototype of which is claimed to have attained 404 m.p.h., was not placed in production, and although no illustrations of the SAM-13 are available, its general description matches that of the twin-engined fighter referred to in the intelligence report. It would seem almost certain, therefore, that the designation MiG-5 was allocated to the single radial-engined fighter evolved by Artem Mikoyan and Mikhail Gurevich.

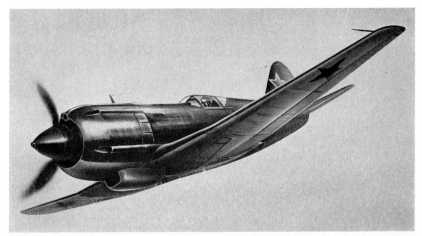

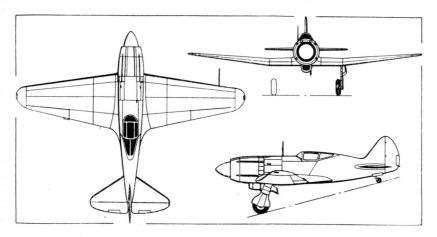

The MiG-5's airframe was essentially that of the preceding MiG-3, the principal changes being those dictated by the replacement of the liquid-cooled Mikulin AM-35A inline engine with a fourteen-cylinder Shvetsov ASh-82 radial air-cooled engine. Like earlier MiG fighters, the MiG-5 was of mixed construction, the rear fuselage and outboard wing sections being of wood and the remainder of metal. Armament comprised four machine guns, two being mounted on each side of the engine, and various underwing loads of RS-82 air-to-surface rockets, 55-lb., 110-lb. or 220-lb. bombs or containers for small anti-personnel bombs could be carried.

Development of the MiG-5 is believed to have been undertaken concurrently with that of Lavochkin's La-5 in 1941, the prototype, a

modified MiG-3 airframe, flying in 1942. The MiG-5 is known to have been in service in small numbers in 1943, but it appears that production was terminated in favour of the superior La-5.

Type: *Single-seat Fighter-bomber.* **Power Plant:** *One 1,600 h.p. Shvetsov M-82A (ASh-82A) fourteen-cylinder radial air-cooled engine.* **Armament:** *Four 7.62-mm. ShKAS machine guns plus six RS-82 rocket projectiles, two 220-lb. or 110-lb. bombs or four 55-lb. bombs.* **Performance:** *Estimated maximum speed, 370 m.p.h. at sea level, 350 m.p.h. at 16,400 ft.* **Weights:** *Approximate loaded, 7,055 lb.* **Dimensions:** *Span, 33 ft. 9½ in.; length, 26 ft. 0 in.; height, 9 ft. 2 in.; wing area, 191.44 sq. ft.*

MIKOYAN-GUREVICH MIG-7

SOVIET UNION

By 1943, the Russians were becoming increasingly concerned over their inability to intercept high-flying Luftwaffe reconnaissance aircraft, and the Protective Air Force, or *Protivovozdushnoi Oborony* (P.V.O.), which had the task of defending specific targets demanded an interceptor capable of operating effectively at altitudes in excess of 40,000 feet. To meet this requirement Artem Mikoyan and Mikhail Gurevich began work on a pressurized high-altitude single-seat fighter, the MiG-7.

The MiG-7 evinced a marked family resemblance to the earlier MiG fighters, and featured a long-span, three-piece wing of relatively high aspect ratio offering high-lift characteristics at extreme altitudes. The inboard leading edges of the wing housed the coolant and oil radiators, and the trailing edges carried long-span flaps. Power was provided by a Klimov M-107A (VK-107A) liquid-cooled inline engine with a multi-stage compressor, the intake for which was positioned beneath the forward fuselage. An inordinately large airscrew with four paddle

The MiG-7 was the only Russian fighter developed during the war to feature a pressure cabin.

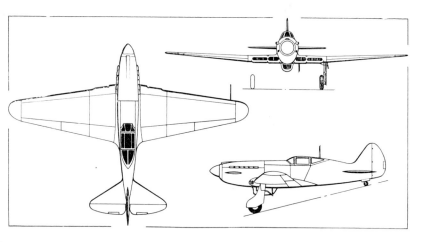

blades was fitted, and a pressure cabin was provided for the pilot. This pressure cabin was the first to be installed in a Russian fighter and is believed to have been a self-contained unit with armoured bulkheads fore and aft, but it is not known what differential pressure was employed. A double windscreen of armour glass was demisted by air which was heated before being led through the space between the inner and outer panels.

The MiG-7 was of all-metal construction with a fully retractable undercarriage, the main members of which were similar to those of the MiG-3 and MiG-5, and were housed entirely within the wing. The first prototype MiG-7 is believed to have commenced flight testing late in 1944, but no production was undertaken as, by this stage in the war, the

danger from high-flying Luftwaffe aircraft had diminished. However, the MiG-7 provided the Soviet aircraft industry with much useful experience with pressure cabin development for incorporation in Russia's first post-war generation of turbojet-powered fighters.

No details of the results of flight tests with the MiG-7 have been revealed.

Type: *Single-seat High-altitude Interceptor.* **Power Plant:** *One* 1,700 *h.p. Klimov M-107A (VK-107A) twelve-cylinder Vee liquid-cooled engine.* **Armament:** *Probably one engine-mounted* 20-*mm. ShVAK cannon and two or four machine guns.* **Performance:** *No details available for publication apart from a service ceiling of* 41,000 *ft.* **Weights:** *No details available.* **Dimensions:** *No details available.*

147

MIKOYAN I-250 (N)   SOVIET UNION

The ramjet, a continuous thermal duct, is mechanically the simplest form of jet propulsion unit. The principle of the ramjet was first propounded in 1913, but at that time it was merely of academic interest owing to the low speeds of aircraft then current. The ramjet depends upon air rammed into a diffuser duct and, for effective operation, demands a velocity of at least 350 m.p.h. With the attainment of such speeds by fighter aircraft, several Russian scientists began to evince an interest in the ramjet as did their contemporaries in other countries, particularly Germany, and a series of small ramjet units was evolved which was intended to boost the power of fighters at the higher speeds and altitudes at which the efficiency of the piston engine and its airscrew

tended to fall away. Some La-7 and La-9 fighters were fitted with a pair of ramjets mounted under the wings, and in 1943 Artem I. Mikoyan began work on a small interceptor fighter designed from the outset for composite power, a twelve-cylinder liquid-cooled piston engine being installed in the nose and a small ramjet being fitted in the rear fuselage.

Designated I-250 (N), the fighter was a low-wing cantilever monoplane of all-metal construction. The VK-107A engine drove a normal three-blade airscrew and also a compressor boosting the flow of air to the ramjet mounted aft. The VK-107A was provided with an annular intake, and the intake for the ramjet was situated in the deepened nose, the ramjet exhausting in the extreme rear fuselage. The

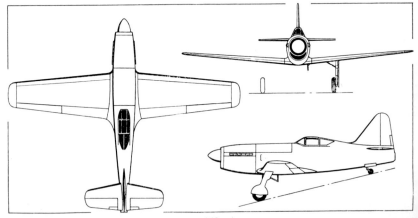

148

prototype I-250 (N) was flown for the first time in March 1945, and during the course of its flight trials exceeded 497 m.p.h. in level flight with both power plants operating. However, by this time Soviet troops had occupied many of Germany's turbojet manufacturing plants, and Soviet technical groups had uncovered many technical documents indicating the tremendous potentialities of the turbojet. In consequence, the further development of the I-250 (N) was abandoned, Artem Mikoyan and his team transferring their attentions to the design of pure jet fighters, such as the MiG-9.

Very few details of the Mikoyan I-250 (N) interceptor were subsequently revealed, and those that follow are derived from official Soviet sources.

Type: *Single-seat Interceptor Fighter.* **Power Plants:** *One 1,600 h.p. Klimov VK-107A twelve-cylinder Vee liquid-cooled engine and one ramjet.* **Armament:** *One 20-mm. ShVAK cannon and two or four 12.7-mm. Beresin BS machine guns.* **Performance:** *Maximum speed, 513 m.p.h.; maximum range, 1,130 mls.; ceiling, 36,745 ft.* **Weights:** *Loaded, 8,113 lb.* **Dimensions:** *No details available for publication.*

NIKITIN-SEVCHENKO IS-1

Perhaps the most novel of the single-seat fighters under test in the Soviet Union at the time of the German onslaught were the IS-1 and IS-2 designed by V. V. Nikitin and V. Sevchenko. In 1939, these designers began to consider ways and means of combining the take-off and landing characteristics and the extreme manoeuvrability of the biplane with the high speed of the monoplane. Their solution to the problem resulted in a unique fighter prototype, the IS-1, which the pilot could transform from biplane to monoplane and vice versa at will!

In order to speed development, Nikitin and Sevchenko adapted the fuselage of a Polikarpov I-153 for their first prototype. To this was fitted a cantilever gull-type upper wing

and a hydraulically *retractable* lower wing. The inboard portions of the lower wing housed the main undercarriage members and were winched up to lie flush in recesses in the fuselage sides, the outer portions being hinged to fit into recesses in the upper wing. The tailplane was lowered and the vertical surfaces enlarged. For take-off the lower wing was locked in the extended position. This was then retracted hydraulically, being extended again for landing. Flight trials proved that the scheme was practicable, although it is likely that some extremely peculiar airflow effects were experienced during the wing retraction and extension phase of each flight, and a more advanced prototype, the IS-2, was completed and flown late in 1940. This

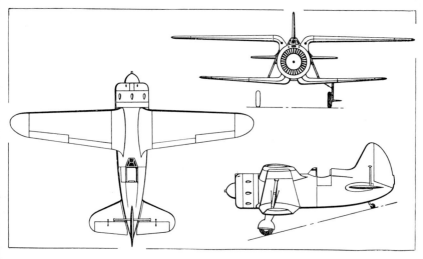

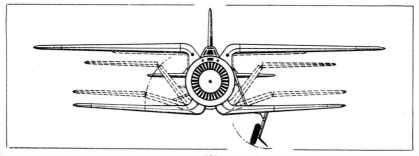

151

differed from its predecessor primarily in having a redesigned fuselage and improved retraction mechanism for the lower wing.

Despite the originality of the scheme and the relative success of flight trials, it was decided that the marginal improvement in performance offered over existing biplanes did not justify the complexity of the fighter's conception. It was considered probable that, under operational conditions, the heavy retraction mechanism and hydraulic system would offer serious maintenance problems, and further development of the IS-2 was abandoned.

The accompanying illustrations depict the IS-1, no illustrations of the later IS-2 having been revealed, and the following specification also relates to the IS-1.

Type: *Single-seat Interceptor Fighter.* **Power Plant:** *One 1,100 h.p. Shvetsov M-63 nine-cylinder radial air-cooled engine.* **Armament:** *Four 7.62-mm. ShKAS machine guns in forward fuselage.* **Performance:** *Estimated maximum speed (in monoplane configuration), 285 m.p.h. at 16,400 ft.; estimated cruising speed (biplane configuration), 180 m.p.h.* **Weights:** *No details available for publication.* **Estimated dimensions:** *Span, 28 ft. 8 in.; length, 20 ft. 0 in.; height, 7 ft. 10 in.*

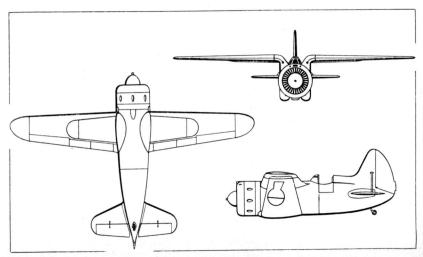

POLIKARPOV I-15

During the summer of 1932, Nikolai N. Polikarpov began work on the design of two new fighters, the TsKB-3, later to become the I-15, which was a logical successor to his successful I-5 biplane of 1930, and the TsKB-12 monoplane which was to enter service as the I-16. At this time, Polikarpov was working at the *Tsentralnii Aerogidrodinamicheskii Institut* (Central Aero and Hydrodynamic Institute), or TsAGI, and the first of the two fighters to fly was the TsKB-3 which made its début in October 1933.

The TsKB-3 was a sesquiplane of mixed construction with single streamlined bracing struts, cantilever undercarriage legs and a 700 h.p. M-25 engine. The upper wing was of gull form, fairing into the fuselage to provide the pilot with an unimpeded forward view,

(*Below*) *The record-breaking I-15 used by Kokkinaki in 1935 to raise the World Altitude Record to 47,818 feet.*

A substantial number of I-15s were used during the Spanish Civil War, a survivor of this conflict being illustrated.

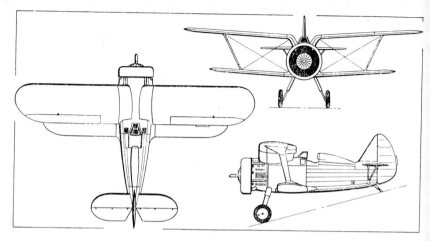

and an armament of four 7.62-mm. machine guns was carried. The TsKB-3 was immediately placed in quantity production and was, by world standards appertaining at the time, an excellent fighter with a good performance and exceptional manoeuvrability. On November 21, 1935, the well-known Russian test pilot V. Kokkinaki raised the World Altitude Record to 47,818 feet while flying a specially modified machine of this type. In Russian service, the fighter was designated I-15, and no less than 550 I-15s and the later I-15bis fighters were shipped to Spain where they fought with the Republicans. In Spain, the I-15 was dubbed *Chato* (the "Flat-nosed One").

By November 30, 1939, when Russian forces attacked Finland, the I-15 was totally obsolete. Nevertheless, a number of VVS-RKKA units engaged in this campaign employed the I-15 which, for winter operations, was mounted on skis, and a small number were employed against the Luftwaffe, principally in the close-support role, during the opening weeks of the German attack.

Type: *Single-seat General-purpose Fighter.* **Power Plant:** *One 700 h.p. M-25 (licence-built Wright Cyclone 9) nine-cylinder radial air-cooled engine.* **Armament:** *Four 7.62-mm. DA or ShKAS machine guns.* **Performance:** *Maximum speed, 224 m.p.h.; maximum cruising speed, 180 m.p.h.; range, 450 mls.; maximum ceiling, 32,800 ft.* **Weights:** *Empty, 2,597 lb.; loaded, 3,135 lb.* **Dimensions:** *Span, 29 ft. 11½ in.; length, 20 ft. 7½ in.; height, 9 ft. 7 in.; wing area, 225 sq ft.*

POLIKARPOV I-15BIS

During 1934, with the I-15 entering production, Polikarpov's design team began work on an improved version of the basic design, the TsKB-3bis or I-15bis. The principal differences between the I-15 and I-15bis were to be seen in the upper wing which was raised above the fuselage by a series of bracing struts and in the long-chord engine cowling which enclosed a 750 h.p. M-25B engine which drove an AV-1 two-blade metal airscrew. The construction of the I-15bis was, like that of its predecessor, mixed wood and steel tube with fabric covering, and the 68 Imp. gal. internal fuel tanks in the fuselage could be supplemented by two 22 Imp. gal. auxiliary tanks which could be slung under the lower wings on the bomb shackles. These normally carried two 110-lb. or four 55-lb. bombs. A 9-mm.

armour plate provided the pilot with rear protection.

The I-15bis served in substantial numbers in Spain, and was also supplied to the Chinese government. It was also used during the fighting between Russo-Mongolian and Japanese forces during the Buir Nuur and Nomonkhan battles on the Manchukuoan border, and still equipped a substantial number of the VVS-RKKA first-line units in 1939–40, being encountered by the Finns. Many aircraft of this type were destroyed by the Luftwaffe during the opening phases of the German assault, but the type had largely disappeared from first-line units by the end of 1941. On January 25, 1940, an I-15bis was flown with two Merkulov ramjets mounted under the lower wing as part of the Soviet experimental

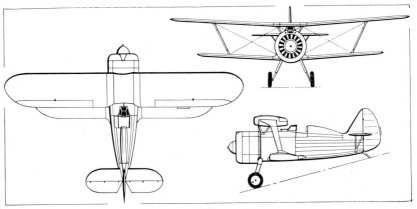

Extensively redesigned by comparison with the original I-15, the I-15bis was used by the Soviet Air Forces during the opening stages of the war. That above was captured by Finnish forces during the 1939-40 "Winter War".

programme concerned with boosting the power of existing types.

Type: *Single-seat General-purpose Fighter-bomber.* **Power Plant:** *One 750 h.p. M-25B (licence-built Wright Cyclone 9) nine-cylinder radial air-cooled engine.* **Armament:** *Four 7.62-mm. ShKAS machine guns with 750 r.p.g. plus six RS-82 rocket missiles, or two 110-lb. or four 55-lb. bombs.* **Performance:** *Maximum speed, 230 m.p.h.; cruising speed, 174 m.p.h.; range, 280 mls. at 186 m.p.h.; range (with two 22 Imp. gal. auxiliary tanks), 497 mls. at 174 m.p.h.; ceiling, 26,245 ft.* **Weights:** *Empty, 2,880 lb.; normal loaded, 3,827 lb.; maximum, 4,189 lb.* **Dimensions,** *Span, 33 ft. 6 in.; length, 20 ft. 9¼ in.; height, 9 ft. 10 in.; wing area, 242 sq. ft.*

POLIKARPOV I-153   SOVIET UNION

The I-153 was unique among serving fighter biplanes in having a retractable undercarriage. It is also probable that the distinction of being the fastest fighter biplane ever to enter service could be claimed for this fighter which first saw action over Spain where it was dubbed the *Chaika* (Gull). Evolved by A. J. Scherbakov from the original I-15 designed by Polikarpov, the I-153 retained the gull-type upper wing which, employed by the original I-15, had been discarded on the I-15bis, and introduced a rearward-retracting undercarriage.

The first prototype I-153, which was flown in 1935, was fitted with a 750 h.p. M-25B

driving an AV-1 two-blade metal airscrew, but the first production series which appeared during the following year employed an 850 h.p. M-62R engine driving an AV-2 airscrew,

(Below) The I-153 in winter finish and (right) being "bombed up".

The I-153 could be fitted with 22 Imp. gal. auxiliary tanks underwing as seen above.

An experimental two-seat variant of the I-153 with enclosed cockpits.

attaining a maximum speed of 249 m.p.h. with this power plant. During the same year a tandem two-seat development with enclosed cockpits was tested, but this model did not attain production status.

The definitive production version of the I-153 was powered by a 1,000 h.p. M-63 engine driving a VV-1 two-blade metal airscrew. The fuselage fuels tanks had a capacity of 68 Imp. gal., but two 22 Imp. gal. auxiliary tanks could be carried on the lower wing, beneath the bracing struts. As with earlier fighters in this series, construction was mixed, the wings being of wood with fabric-covering, and the fuselage being of wood and steel-tube with metal skinning forward and fabric covering aft.

The I-153 was extremely manoeuvrable and was employed extensively by the VVS-RKKA during the Finnish campaign of 1939–40. It served extensively in the Far East and was also encountered in numbers on the Eastern Front by the Luftwaffe.

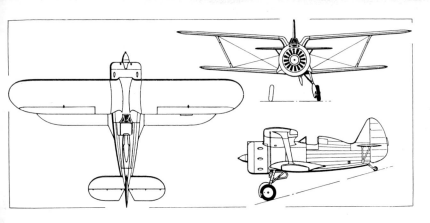

159

Type: *Single-seat Fighter-bomber.* **Power Plant:** *One 1,000 h.p. M-63 (derived from the Wright Cyclone 9) nine-cylinder radial air-cooled engine.* **Armament:** *Four 7.62-mm. ShKAS machine guns with 650 r.p.g. plus six RS-82 rocket missiles or two 165-lb. bombs.* **Performance:** *Maximum speed, 267 m.p.h. at 16,400 ft.; cruising speed, 186 m.p.h.; range (internal fuel), 298 mls. at 186 m.p.h. (with two 22 Imp. gal. auxiliary tanks), 560 mls. at 174 m.p.h.; ceiling, 35,145 ft.* **Weights:** *Empty, 3,168 lb.; normal loaded, 4,100 lb.; maximum, 4,431 lb.* **Dimensions:** *Span, 32 ft. 9¾ in.; length, 20 ft. 3¼ in.; height, 9 ft. 3 in.; wing area, 238 sq. ft.*

An I-153 fighter taking-off on the Eastern Front during the early months of the German attack.

(Below) One of several I-153 fighters captured by Finnish forces. This type was extremely manœuvrable.

POLIKARPOV I-16

SOVIET UNION

The I-16 single-seat monoplane fighter designed by a team headed by Nikolai N. Polikarpov was obsolete at the beginning of the Second World War, yet it bore much of the brunt of the early Luftwaffe offensive against the Soviet Union and continued in first-line service until 1943. It possessed the distinction of being the first low-wing interceptor monoplane with a retractable undercarriage to enter service anywhere in the world! It was, despite some crudity of equipment and construction by western standards appertaining at the time, of very advanced conception. It was strongly built, capable of withstanding considerable punishment, easily maintained, and, at the time of its service début, faster than any of its foreign contemporaries. It was claimed at one time that Polikarpov drew his inspiration for the I-16 from the American Boeing P-26, but in fact the Russian fighter did not bear the remotest resemblance to the American fighter, and was actually under test before the first P-26A was delivered to the U.S. Army Air Corps.

(*Below and right*) *I-16 Type 24 fighters. These were the most numerous of Soviet warplanes during the first year of the war.*

(Above and left) Ski-equipped *I-16 Type 24 fighters captured by Finnish forces.*

Design work on the fighter that was eventually to enter service as the I-16 began during the summer of 1932 at the *Tsentralnii Aerogidrodinamicheskii Institut* (Central Aero and Hydrodynamic Institute), or TsAGI, and the first prototype, designated TsKB-12, flew for the first time in December 1933. Powered by a 480 h.p. M-22 radial (licence-built Gnôme-et-Rhône Jupiter), the TsKB-12 was of mixed construction with a manually-operated, inward-retracting undercarriage, and two 7.62-mm. guns fired through the airscrew disc. As a result of successful trials, production of the fighter was immediately initiated by factories No. 1 and No. 21 at Moscow and Gorki respectively.

The initial production model of the I-16, which received the TsAGI designation TsKB-12bis, was powered by a 775 h.p. M-25B radial derived from the Wright Cyclone 9, and attained a maximum speed of 283 m.p.h. as compared with 224 m.p.h. for the first prototype. The initial production series were designated I-16 Types 4, 5 and 10—the "type" suffixes indicating equipment changes—and these had the M-25B radial driving an AV-1 two-blade metal airscrew and carried an armament of four 7.62-mm. ShKAS machine guns with a total of 900 rounds. These early production models had average empty and loaded weights of 2,791 lb. and 3,704 lb. respectively. Maximum and cruising speeds were 283 m.p.h. and 224 m.p.h.; the internal fuel capacity of 56 Imp. gal. provided a cruising range of 400 mls., and the ceiling was 29,500 ft. One of these early production I-16s was acquired by the Japanese Army Air Force at the beginning of 1940 when a Mongolian pilot, claiming political asylum, landed his I-16 at Arutaukou in eastern Manchuria. The fighter was extensively tested by the J.A.A.F., and Major G. Yamamoto who flew the I-16 in comparative trials with Japanese fighters said that the "Russian fighter was insensitive by comparison with Japanese fighters, and its c.g. was too far aft, resulting in serious elevator heaviness." He added that the nose of the Russian fighter rose alarmingly as soon as the flaps were lowered for landing, and that it was extremely difficult to wind up the undercarriage.

The Soviet government took the opportunity presented by the Spanish Civil War to evaluate the I-16 under operational conditions, the first fighters of this type arriving at Carta-

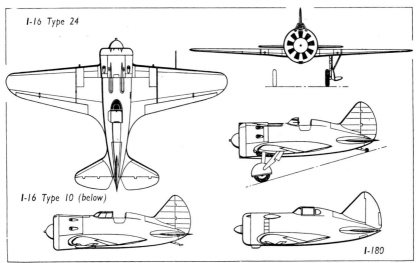

I-16 Type 24

I-16 Type 10 (below)

I-180

A late-production M-25-powered I-16. This fighter was of extremely advanced conception at the time of its début.

gena in October 1936, joining combat during the following month with pilots of the *Brigadas Internacionales*. In Spain, the I-16 was dubbed *Mosca* (Fly) by its pilots and *Rata* (Rat) by its opponents. A year later, when the I-16 appeared in Chinese skies and on the Mongolian-Siberian-Manchurian borders, it was dubbed the *Abu* (Gadfly) by the Japanese. Russian "volunteer" squadrons operated the I-16 over China where it proved fairly evenly matched with the Mitsubishi A5M2a fighters of the Japanese Navy, the Russian fighter having the edge in maximum level and dive speeds, and the Japanese fighter possessing superior manoeuvrability. The 9-mm. armour plate which gave rear protection to the pilot of the I-16 could not be penetrated by the standard Japanese 7.7-mm. or 12.7-mm. ammunition. By the time the Spanish Civil War came to an end in March 1939, a total of 475 I-16 fighters had been sent to Spain,

together with four examples of the tandem two-seat UT I-16 trainer.

Attempts to improve the effectiveness of the I-16 included the TsKB-18 which carried six 7.62-mm. PV-1 machine guns and was intended primarily for close-support duties. The I-16 Type 17 appeared in 1938, and this variant, carrying two wing-mounted 20-mm. ShVAK cannon and two fuselage-mounted 7.62-mm. ShKAS guns, was manufactured in very large numbers. One experimental model, the TsKB-12P (the "P" suffix indicating *Pushka*, or Cannon), had two fuselage-mounted ShVAK cannon firing through the airscrew disc. The final version to be built in substantial quantities was the I-16 Type 24 powered by an M-62 or M-62R radial driving an AV-2 two-blade airscrew. Among late variants were the TsKB-29 which differed primarily in having a pneumatically-retractable undercarriage, and the I-16 SPB dive-bomber. The two-seat I-16UTI, also known as the UTI-4, was produced in substantial numbers, largely by the conversion of early production fighters, and according to German wartime reports, a single-seat model with a 1,100 h.p. M-63 engine appeared in 1942. Luftwaffe pilots who tested captured I-16 fighters reported that they were extremely manoeuvrable but that longitudinal stability was poor. A modernised version of the basic design, the I-180, was evolved in 1938 but did not attain production status. The I-180 was powered by a 1,100 h.p. M-88 air-cooled radial and featured an enclosed cockpit. Maximum speed was 342 m.p.h.

The following relates to the I-16 Type 24.

Type: *Single-seat Fighter-bomber.* **Power Plant:** *One* 1,000 *h.p. Shvetsov M-62 nine-cylinder radial air-cooled engine.* **Armament:** *Two 20-mm. ShVAK cannon with 180 r.p.g. and two 7.62-mm. ShKAS machine guns with 450 r.p.g., plus six RS-82 rocket missiles or two VAP-6M or ZAP-6 chemical containers.* **Performance:** *Maximum speed, 326 m.p.h. at sea level, 286 m.p.h. at 14,765 ft.; economic cruising speed, 186 m.p.h.; range (56 Imp. gal. internally), 250 mls., (plus two 22 Imp. gal. auxiliary tanks) 435 mls.; ceiling, 29,530 ft.* **Weights:** *Empty, 3,285 lb.; normal loaded, 4,189 lb.; maximum, 4,520 lb.* **Dimensions:** *Span, 29 ft. 6½ in.; length, 20 ft. 1¼ in.; height, 8 ft. 5 in.; wing area, 161 sq. ft.*

The I-16 fighter (an M-25-powered version of which is illustrated) was extremely manœuvrable but had poor longitudinal stability.

POLIKARPOV I-17

SOVIET UNION

Nikolai N. Polikarpov's I-17-1, or TsKB-15, has been claimed by Soviet propagandists to have been the prototype for international fighter construction; the progenitor of the fast, single-seat, low-wing fighter monoplane with a liquid-cooled engine and a retractable undercarriage. In fact, work on such aircraft was proceeding simultaneously in several countries, but the I-17 *did* fly some nine months earlier than any of its contemporaries as a result of Polikarpov's remarkable feat of designing and building the fighter in less than eight months!

Flown for the first time on September 1, 1934, the first prototype, the I-17-1 or TsKB-15, was designed at the TsAGI and, although

of exceptionally advanced conception, featured a rather complex all-metal structure, the wings having a single tubular main spar and the fuselage being entirely of steel tube with riveted metal skin. The I-17-1 was powered by an imported 840 h.p. Hispano-Suiza 12Y liquid-cooled Vee engine, but the second prototype, the I-17-2 or TsKB-19, was powered by the Russian-built version of the Hispano-Suiza 12Y, the 860 h.p. M-100 which had been modified by V. I. Klimov. The armament of the second machine comprised one engine-mounted cannon of 20-mm. calibre and four wing-mounted 7.62-mm. machine guns, whereas the first prototype carried two 20-mm. cannon and two 7.62-mm. machine

The I-17-2 (TsKB-19) illustrated below was the first prototype powered by the M-100 engine.

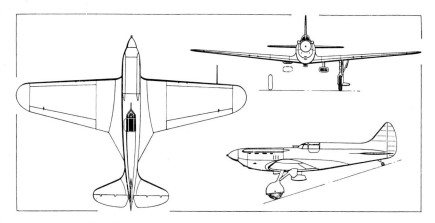

guns all mounted in the wings. The second prototype was displayed at the 1936 Paris International Aeronautical Exhibition where the generally poor workmanship of the aircraft and the heavy and crudely finished engine received much comment.

Prior to the I-17's début in Paris further development of the basic design had already been undertaken, and a third prototype, designated TsKB-33, had flown. This embodied some minor structural refinements and a reduced armament of three 7.62-mm. guns. In 1937, Polikarpov adapted the fighter for launching from TB-3 heavy bombers, this variant being designated I-17-Z. The I-17-Z, which featured wings of reduced span and area, was to have been slung beneath the outboard wing sections of the bomber, but development was abandoned.

Limited production of the I-17 was undertaken during 1937–39, and, although there is no record of the I-17 being encountered by the Luftwaffe, it remained in service with several VVS-RKKA units until 1942, fighters of this type being encountered by the Hungarian Air Force.

Type: *Single-seat Interceptor and Fighter-bomber.* **Power Plant:** *One 860 h.p. Klimov M-100 twelve-cylinder Vee liquid-cooled engine.* **Armament:** *One 20-mm. ShVAK cannon and two 7.62-mm. ShKAS machine guns, plus two 110-lb. or four 55-lb. bombs.* **Performance:** *Maximum speed, 305 m.p.h.; maximum cruising speed, 273 m.p.h.; economic cruising speed, 246 m.p.h.; range, 497 mls. at 246 m.p.h. at 16,400 ft.; endurance, 2 hrs.; initial climb rate, 3,400 ft./min.; ceiling, 36,090 ft.* **Weights:** *Empty, 3,770 lb.; normal loaded, 4,220 lb.* **Dimensions:** *Span, 33 ft. 1⅞ in.; length, 24 ft. 3½ in.; height, 8 ft. 5 in.; wing area, 190.5 sq. ft.*

The first fighter to be designed by Alexander S. Yakovlev, dubbed the *Krasavec* (Beauty) and initially designated I-26, was flown for the first time in the summer of 1940, being displayed publicly on November 7, 1940 during the course of an Air Fête held near Moscow. Such was the success of the prototype that Yakovlev was immediately awarded the Order of Lenin, a Zis car and 100,000 roubles. Redesignated Yak-1, the fighter entered production a few weeks before the German onslaught began in June 1941, and in the remarkably short period of nine months was re-equipping VVS-RKKA units.

The Yak-1 was of mixed construction with a two-spar wooden wing, a mixed steel-tube and wood fuselage and a plywood skin which was covered with fabric and coated with a thick layer of polish. A Klimov M-105PA drove a VISh-61P three-blade metal airscrew, and fuel was housed in four wing tanks with a total capacity of 90 Imp. gal. Armament comprised a single 20-mm. ShVAK engine-mounted cannon and two fuselage-mounted 7.62-mm. ShKAS machine guns. The initial production model differed little externally from the prototype, apart from having the oil cooler moved forward under the nose, the cockpit canopy redesigned and a modified undercarriage, but improvements were progressively introduced on the production line. One of the first changes was the replacement of the twin ShKAS machine guns with a pair of 12.7-mm. Beresin BS guns with a total of 695 rounds and an increase in the capacity of the cannon shell tanks from 120 to 140 rounds. The VISh-61P airscrew was then supplanted by an automatic VISh-105SV, and in one production batch designated Yak-1M (the "M" suffix indicating *Modificatsion*, or Modification), the rear fuselage was cut down and a three-piece all-round-vision hood fitted. Subsequently, the 1,260 h.p. M-105-PF engine replaced the lower-powered M-105PA, and with the standardisation of all these modifications, the fighter was redesignated Yak-7B.

At an early stage in the development of the design a tandem two-seat variant was evolved for conversion training and high-speed liaison, and originally designated UTI-26, this entered

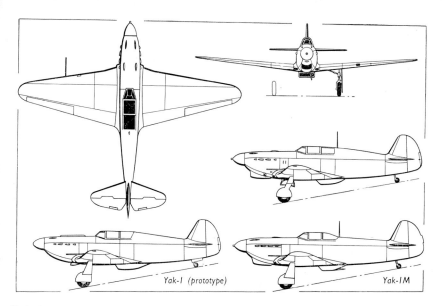

Yak-1 (prototype)

Yak-1M

limited production as the Yak-1U. With the more powerful M-105PF engine and cut-down rear fuselage it became the Yak-7U. Apart from range, the performance of the Yak-7B single-seat fighter was generally similar to that of the Yak-9 described on the following pages, and the following specification relates to the initial production Yak-1.

Type: *Single-seat General-purpose Fighter and Fighter-bomber.* **Power Plant:** *One 1,100 h.p. Klimov M-105PA (VK-105PA) twelve-cylinder Vee liquid-cooled engine.* **Armament:** *One 20-mm. ShVAK cannon with 120 rounds and two 7.62-mm. ShKAS machine guns with 375 r.p.g., plus six RS-82 rocket missiles.* **Performance:** *Maximum speed, 310 m.p.h. at sea level, 364 m.p.h. at 16,400 ft.; economical cruising speed, 155 m.p.h. at sea level, 149 m.p.h. at 9,840 ft.; range, 435 mls. at 323 m.p.h.; time to 16,400 ft., 4 min. 30 sec.; service ceiling, 32,800 ft.* **Weights:** *Empty, 5,137 lb.; loaded, 6,217 lb.* **Dimensions:** *Span, 32 ft. 9¾ in.; length, 27 ft. 9¼ in.; height, 8 ft. 8 in.; wing area, 184.5 sq. ft.*

YAKOVLEV YAK-9

While the Yak-7B was being delivered to the VVS-RKKA a further development of the basic design, the Yak-9, was being readied for production. Among the shortcomings of the Yak-1 and Yak-7B was a relatively short range at operational cruising speeds, and the wings of the Yak-9 differed from those of the earlier fighters in having metal spars which permitted the installation of larger fuel cells. The cockpit was moved aft and the ventral radiator bath was moved forward. The Klimov M-105PF engine was similar to that of the Yak-7B, and deliveries to the VVS-RKKA began in August 1942, the type making its operational début during the fighting in the vicinity of Stalingrad in the following October.

Two variants appeared in 1943, the Yak-9D (the "D" suffix indicating *Dalnaya*, or Range), and the Yak-9T (the "T" indicating *Tankov* and referring to its large calibre cannon for anti-tank duties). The Yak-9D had its forward-firing armament reduced to one 20-mm. ShVAK cannon with 120 rounds and one 12.7-mm. BS machine gun with 220 rounds, and the fuel capacity was increased to 132

Yak-9D fighters of the type used to escort U.S.A.A.F. bombers on their shuttle raids.

170

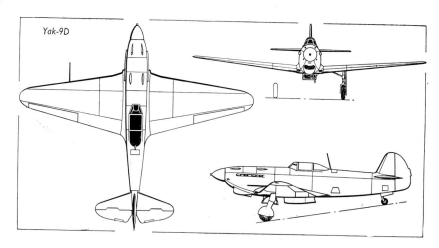

Yak-9D

Imp. gal. The Yak-9D was allocated the task of escorting U.S.A.A.F. heavy bombers on the shuttle raids between the United Kingdom, the Soviet Union and Italy. The Yak-9D had a maximum endurance of 4 hr. 7 min., and a maximum range of 882 miles at 177–193 m.p.h. at 1,640–3,280 ft. At 248 m.p.h. at 9,840 ft. the range and endurance were 675 mls. and 2 hr. 10 min. respectively.

The Yak-9T was produced in two versions, the principal production variant having a single 37-mm. Nudelman-Suranov NS cannon with 30 rounds and a single 12.7-mm. BS gun with 220 rounds for aiming purposes. A second version carried a single 75-mm. cannon and was tested with limited success against enemy armour and against shipping in the Black Sea. Other production variants of the

basic design were the Yak-9L and Yak-9M, but exact details of the changes embodied in these models are unknown. It is believed, however, that they were confined to armament and minor equipment modifications.

The Yak-9 was used by the Polish 1st Fighter Regiment Warszawa which began operations with the VVS-RKKA in August 1944, and by the French Groupe de Chasse GC 3 (Normandie-Niemen) which had joined combat on the Eastern Front in March 1943. By far the larger part of the 30,000 Yakovlev fighters produced during the war (half of these being produced by one immense plant, Factory No. 153 in the Urals) were Yak-9s. The type was extremely popular with its pilots, possessing particularly light and effective ailerons, and it was in its element at low altitudes where

(Above and left) An early production Yak-9 with a 12.7-mm. gun mounted between the cylinder banks in place of the usual cannon.

it could out-turn any opposing fighters. It lacked the refinements of its western contemporaries, and much of its equipment was crude and rudimentary, but it was undoubtedly a most effective combat aircraft by any standard.

The following specification relates specifically to the Yak-9T.

Type: *Single-seat Close-support Fighter.* **Power Plant:** *One 1,260 h.p. Klimov M-105PF (VK-105PF) twelve-cylinder Vee liquid-cooled engine.* **Armament:** *One 37-mm. Nudelman-Suranov NS cannon with 30 rounds and one 12.7-mm. Beresin BS machine gun with 220 rounds.* **Performance:** *Maximum speed, 310 m.p.h. at sea level, 329 m.p.h. at 7,220 ft., 363 m.p.h. at 16,400 ft.; maximum cruising speed, 292 m.p.h.; economic cruising speed, 177 m.p.h.; range, 516 mls. at 177 m.p.h. at 3,280 ft.; service ceiling, 36,090 ft.* **Weights:** *Empty, 6,063 lb.; loaded, 7,055 lb.* **Dimensions:** *Span, 32 ft. 9¾ in.; length, 28 ft. 0½ in.; height, 8 ft. 0 in.; wing area, 185.676 sq. ft.*

YAKOVLEV YAK-9U

SOVIET UNION

In 1944, Alexander Yakovlev's design bureau began work on a "second generation" series of fighters, the first of which was the Yak-9U which was in production during the closing stages of the war but was too late to see operational service. Whereas the "first generation" Yak-9s featured a wing of mixed construction comprising two duralumin spars with wooden ribs covered by plywood, and a welded steel-tube fuselage with metal covering over the forward and centre portions (along the top of the fuselage to a point just aft of the cockpit and along the underside to a point aft of the radiator bath) and fabric covering aft with a wooden tail assembly, the Yak-9U adopted an all-metal structure with metal stressed skinning. This change was accompanied by the installation of the 1,650 h.p.

Klimov M-107A (VK-107A) with a two-stage supercharger, and it was to this increase in power that the suffix "U" referred. Whereas previously this letter had invariably indicated a training variant, on the Yak-9U it indicated *Usilennui*, or "strengthened".

By comparison with earlier versions of the Yak-9, the Yak-9U differed externally in having cleaner nose contours, the oil cooler

Virtually a new aircraft, the Yak-9U was too late to see operational service but was used by Russian and "satellite" units in the post-war years.

173

intake being transferred from under the nose to the port wing root, the starboard wing root being occupied by the carburettor air intake. The cockpit canopy was revised, and the breeches of the 12.7-mm. BS guns necessitated bulges in the fuselage panelling forward of the cockpit. All fuel was housed in four wing tanks which had a total capacity of 132 Imp. gal.

The Yak-9U was one of the first Russian fighters to compare favourably from the structural viewpoint with its western counterparts, and it was to remain in service with many first-line units of the VVS-SA until the early 'fifties. It was also to see service with several of the air arms of Russia's "satellite" countries, the final production model being the Yak-9P which featured additional navigational and radio aids and differed externally from the Yak-9U in having a transparent panel in the rear fuselage covering a D/F loop.

Type: *Single-seat Interceptor and Fighter-bomber.* **Power Plant:** *One 1,650 h.p. Klimov M-107A (VK-107A) twelve-cylinder Vee liquid-cooled engine.* **Armament:** *One 20-mm. ShVAK cannon with 100 rounds and two 12.7-mm. Beresin BS machine guns with 250 r.p.g., plus two 220-lb. bombs.* **Performance:** *Maximum speed, 415 m.p.h. at 16,400 ft.; cruising speed, 300 m.p.h.; range, 506 mls. at 300 m.p.h., 575 mls. at 242 m.p.h.; service ceiling, 34,000 ft.* **Weights:** *Empty, 5,100 lb.; loaded, 6,985 lb.* **Dimensions:** *Span, 32 ft. 9¾ in.; length, 28 ft. 6½ in.; height, 8 ft. 0 in.; wing area, 185.676 sq. ft.*

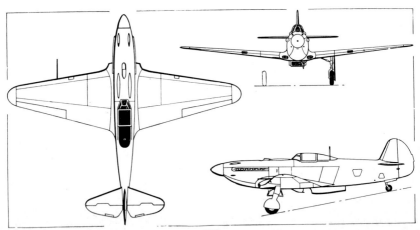

YAKOVLEV YAK-3

SOVIET UNION

Developed in parallel with the Yak-9, the Yak-3 was designed specifically for low-altitude combat and army co-operation. Introduced in 1944, the Yak-3 employed mixed construction and had an exceptionally fine finish achieved by applying a thick layer of polish. The Yak-3 differed from the Yak-9 in having a smaller wing span and area and the oil cooler intake in the port wing root. Pilots that flew both the Yak-3 and the early versions of the Spitfire claimed that the Russian fighter was lighter on the ailerons, smoother to fly, and possessed superior speed and initial climb. It usually operated at altitudes below 8,000–11,000 feet at which it was markedly superior to both the

(Above and opposite page) A Yak-3 of the French Normandie-Niemen Groupe de Chasse during the last months of the war.

Bf 109G and Fw 190A, and it was extensively used for ground strafing. The Yak-3 also served as an escort for Pe-2 and Il-2 bombers, one formation of the fighters accompanying the bombers and another attacking enemy airfields in the area some minutes before the arrival of the bombers.

In addition to serving with regiments of the VVS-RKKA, the Yak-3 was supplied to both the Polish 1st Fighter Regiment Warszawa and the Normandie-Niemen Groupe de Chasse, supplanting their Yak-9s. Both armour and armament were light by western standards, the former being restricted to 9-mm. plate aft of the pilot. Like the other wartime Yakovlev fighters, the Yak-3 was rugged, light, austerely equipped and easy to build. Its stalling speed was on the high side, and it could reportedly

provide a novice with some difficulties during take-off and landing, but in general its flying characteristics were, like those of other Yakovlev fighters, superlative.

Type: *Single-seat Close-support Fighter.* **Power Plant:** *One 1,222 h.p. Klimov M-105PF-2 (VK-105PF-2) twelve-cylinder Vee liquid-cooled engine.* **Armament:** *One 20-mm. ShVAK cannon with 120 rounds and two 12.7-mm. Beresin BS machine guns with 250 r.p.g.* **Performance:** *Maximum speed, 403 m.p.h. at 16,400 ft.; range, 506 mls. at 305 m.p.h., 456 mls. at 341 m.p.h., 560 mls. at 193 m.p.h.; maximum endurance, 2 hr. 55 min.; time to 16,400 ft., 4 min. 30 sec.; ceiling, 35,475 ft.* **Weights:** *Loaded, 5,864 lb.* **Dimensions,** *Span, 30 ft. 2¼ in.; length, 27 ft. 10¾ in.; height, 7 ft. 10 in.*

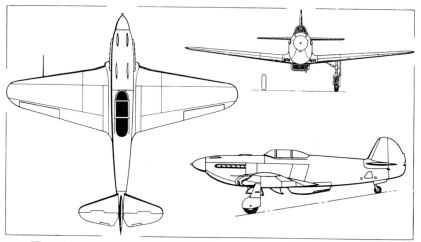

YATSENKO I-28

During the mid-'thirties, the Soviet aircraft industry was abreast, and, in some cases, ahead of its foreign contemporaries in single-seat fighter design, largely as a result of the efforts of Nikolai N. Polikarpov. The Soviet Union was the first country to place in quantity service cantilever fighter monoplanes with retractable undercarriages, but by 1938 the service introduction of such types as the Hawker Hurricane and the Messerschmitt Bf 109 indicated that Russian fighters were falling behind world standards. The highest priority was, therefore, allocated to the design and development of new fighters, and several new designers made their appearance, one of which was V. P. Yatsenko.

The first of the new fighters to appear was the I-22 (later to become the LaGG-1), designed by Semyon A. Lavochkin who was assisted by engineers Gorbunov and Gudkov, this flying for the first time on March 30, 1939. The I-22 was followed closely by the I-28 designed by V. P. Yatsenko. The I-28 was a neat low-wing cantilever monoplane with inward-retracting main undercarriage members and powered by a close-cowled fourteen-cylinder M-87A air-cooled radial rated at 950 h.p. for take-off. The methods of construction adopted by Yatsenko were similar to those employed for the I-22, the entire airframe being built from plastic-bonded wood. The fuselage of the I-28 was built up on birch frames and the skin was composed of diagonal strips of plywood, phenol-formaldehyde resin

178

being used as an adhesive and as an impregnating medium. The three-section wings comprised two box-section spars with plywood skinning, and had a gross area of 177.5 sq. ft. and a loading of 33.07 lb./sq. ft. The centre section was of reverse gull form, and the mainwheels were partly housed in the fuselage. The entire armament of four ShKAS machine guns was housed in the forward fuselage.

Prototypes of the I-28 were still under test when German forces invaded the Soviet Union, but by this time the decision to discontinue development of the M-87A engine and the superior qualities evinced by contemporary designs with liquid-cooled engines had resulted in a diminishing of interest in Yatsenko's fighter, and no production was undertaken.

Very few details have been revealed concerning the characteristics of the Yatsenko I-28, and the following are quoted from official Soviet sources.

Type: *Single-seat Interceptor Fighter and Fighter-bomber.* **Power Plant:** *One 950 h.p. Shvetsov M-87A fourteen-cylinder radial air-cooled engine.* **Armament:** *Four 7.62-mm. ShKAS machine guns mounted in the fuselage and firing through the airscrew disc.* **Performance:** *Maximum speed, 339 m.p.h.* **Weights:** *Loaded, 5,878 lb.* **Dimensions:** *Span, length, height, no details available for publication; wing area, 177.5 sq. ft.*

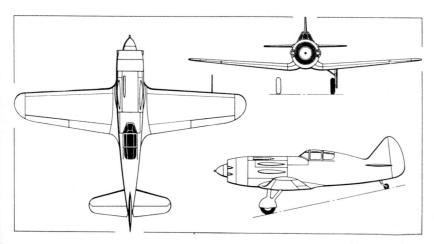

INDEX TO AIRCRAFT TYPES

A5M4, Mitsubishi 40–2
A6M1-3 Zero-Sen, Mit-
  subishi 43–6
A6M5-8 Zero-Sen, Mitsu-
  bishi 47–50
A7M1-2 Reppu, Mitsubishi..51–2
Berezniak-Isaev BI-1 125–6
BI-1, Berezniak-Isaev 125–6
Claude, Mitsubishi A5M4 ...40–2
D.XXI, Fokker 100–3
D.XXIII, Fokker 108–9
De Schelde S.21 98–9
F.K.58, Koolhoven 110–13
Fokker D.XXI 100–3
  D.XXIII 108–9
  G.I 104–7
Frances 26, Kawanishi
  P1Y2-S 10–11
Frank, Nakajima Ki.84 79–83
Hayabusa, Nakajima Ki.43 ..70–5
Hayate, Nakajima Ki.84 ...79–83
Hien, Kawasaki Ki.61 19–24
I-15, Polikarpov 153–4
I-15bis, Polikarpov 155–6
I-16, Polikarpov 161–5
I-17, Polikarpov........166–7
I-22, Lavochkin 127–30
I-26, Yakovlev 168–9
I-28, Yatsenko 178–9
I-61, Mikoyan-Gurevich....140–1
I-153, Polikarpov.......157–9
I-200, Mikoyan-Gurevich ..142–3
I-250 (N), Mikoyan 148–9
I-301, Lavochkin 127–30
I.A.R.80 123–4

I.A.R.81 123–4
Irving, Nakajima J1N1-S ..84–7
IS-1, Nikitin-Sevchenko ...150–1
IS-2, Nikitin-Sevchenko ...150–1
J1N1-S Gekko, Nakajima ..84–7
J2M2-7, Raiden, Mitsubishi .53–7
J5N1 Tenrai, Nakajima 88–9
J7W1 Shinden, Kyushu ...38–9
J8M1 Shusui, Mitsubishi ..62–5
Jack, Mitsubishi J2M2-7 53–7
Jastrzab, PZL P.50 120–2
Ki-38, Kawasaki 12–16
Ki.27, Nakajima 66–9
Ki.43 Hayabusa, Nakajima ..70–5
Ki.44 Shoki, Nakajima.....76–8
Ki.45 Toryu, Kawasaki ...12–16
Ki.60, Kawasaki 17–18
Ki.61 Hien, Kawasaki 19–24
Ki.64, Kawasaki 25–6
Ki.83, Mitsubishi 58–9
Ki.84 Hayate, Nakajima ..79–83
Ki.87, Nakajima 90–1
Ki.93, Rikugun 94–5
Ki.94-II, Tachikawa 96–7
Ki.95, Mitsubishi 58–9
Ki.96, Kawasaki 27–8
Ki.100, Kawasaki 29–32
Ki.102, Kawasaki 33–35
Ki.106, Tachikawa 79–83
Ki.108, Kawasaki 36–7
Ki.109, Mitsubishi.........60–1
Ki.116, Mansyu 79–83
Ki.200, Mitsubishi.......62–4
Kawanishi N1K1-J Shiden ...4–6
  N1K2-J Shiden-Kai 7–9
  P1Y2-S Kyokko 10–11

Kawasaki Ki.45 Toryu 12–16
  Ki.60 17–18
  Ki.61 Hien 19–24
  Ki.64 25–6
  Ki.96 27–8
  Ki.100 29–32
  Ki.102 33–5
  Ki.108 36–7
Koolhoven F.K.58 110–13
Kyokko, Kawanishi P1Y2-S 10–11
Kyushu J7W1 Shinden 38–9
Lavochkin La-5 131–4
  La-7 135–7
  La-9 138–9
  LaGG-3 127–30
Malyutka, Polikarpov.....125–6
Mansyu Ki.116 79–83
Mikoyan I-250 (N) 148–9
Mikoyan-Gurevich MiG-1..140–1
  MiG-3 142–3
  MiG-5 144–5
  MiG-7 146–7
Mitsubishi A5M4 40–2
  A6M1-3 Zero-Sen.....43–6
  A6M5-8 Zero-Sen ...47–50
  A7M1 Reppu 51–2
  J2M2-7 Raiden 53–7
  J8M1 Shusyi 62–5
  Ki.83 58–9
  Ki.109 60–1
  Ki.200 62–5
N1K1-J Shiden, Kawanishi...4–6
N1K2-J Shiden-Kai,
  Kawanishi...............7–9

180

Nakajima J1N1-S Gekko ...84–7
   J5N1 Tenrai 88–9
   Ki.27 66–9
   Ki.43 Hayabusa 70–5
   Ki.44 Shoki 76–8
   Ki.84 Hayate 79–83
   Ki. 87 90–1
Nate, Nakajima Ki.27 66–9
Nick, Kawasaki Ki.45 12–16
Nikitin-Sevchenko IS-1 ...150–1
   IS-2 150–1
Oscar, Nakajima Ki.43.....70–5
P1Y2-S Kyokko, Kawanishi 10–11
Polikarpov I-15 153–4
   I-15bis 155–6
   I-16 161–5
   I-17 166–7
   I-153 157–9
   Malyutka 125–6
PZL P.11 114–16
   P.24 117–19
   P.50 Jastrzab 120–2

Reppu, Mitsubishi A7M1-2..51–2
Rikugun Ki.46-III-KAI 92–3
   Ki.93 94–5
Rob, Kawasaki Ki.64 25–6
S.21, De Schelde 98–9
Sam, Mitsubishi A7M1-2 ...51–2
Shiden, Kawanish ¡N1K1-J...4–6
Shiden-Kai, Kawanishi
   N1K2-J 7–9
Shinden, Kyushu J7W1 38–9
Shoki, Nakajima Ki.44......76–8
Shusui, Mitsubishi J8M1 ...62–5
Tachikawa Ki.94-II 96–7
   Ki.106 79–83
Tenrai, Nakajima J5N1 88–9
Tikhonravov 302 125–6
Tojo, Nakajima Ki.44 76–8
Tony, Kawasaki Ki.61 19–24
Toryu, Kawasaki Ki.45 12–16

TsKB-3, Polikarpov 153–5
TsKB-3bis, Polikarpov 155–6
TsKB-18, Polikarpov 161–5
TsKB-12bis, Polikarpov ...161–5
TsKB-18, Polikarpov 161–5
TsKB-15, Polikarpov 166–7
TsKB-19, Polikarpov 166–7
UTI-4, Polikarpov.........161–5
UTI-26, Yakovlev 168–9
Yakovlev Yak-1...........168–9
   Yak-3 175–7
   Yak-7B 168–9
   Yak-9D 170–2
   Yak-9T 170–2
   Yak-9U 173–4
Yatsenko I-28 178–9
Zeke, Mitsubishi A6M1-8 ..43–50
Zero-Sen, Mitsubishi
   A6M1-3................43–6
Zero-Sen, Mitsubishi
   A6M5-8 47–50